Intra Muros

Christian Memories of Death, Bereavement and the Heavenly Afterlife

By Rebecca Ruter Springer

Published by Pantianos Classics

ISBN-13: 978-1729797617

First published in 1898

Contents

Author's Preface

The pages of this little volume contain no fancy sketch, written to while away an idle hour; but are the true, though greatly condensed, record of an experience during days when life hung in the balance between Time and Eternity, with the scales dipping decidedly toward the Eternity side.

I am painfully aware of the fact that I can never paint for others the scenes as they appeared to me during those wonderful days. If I can only dimly show the close linking of the two lives—the mortal with the divine—as they then appeared to me, I may be able to partly tear the veil from the death we so dread, and show it to be only an open door into a new and beautiful phase of the life we now live.

If any of the scenes depicted should seem irreverent in view of our religious training here, I can only say, "I give it as it came to me." In those strange, happy hours the close blending of the two lives, so wrapped about with the Father's watchful care and tender love; the reunion of friends, with the dear earth-ties unchanged; the satisfied desires, the glad surprises and the divine joys, all intensified and illumined by the reverence and love and adoration that all hearts gave to the blessed Trinity, appeared to me the most perfect revelation of that "blessed life" of which here we so fondly dream. With the hope that it may comfort and uplift some who read, even as it then did, and as its memory ever will do, for me, I submit this imperfect sketch of a most perfect vision.

R.R.S.

"Shall we stop at that poor line, the grave, which all our Christianity is always trying to wipe out and make nothing of, and which we always insist on widening into a great gulf? Shall we not stretch our thought beyond, and feel the life-blood of this holy church, this living body of Christ, pulsing out into the saints who are living there, and coming back throbbing with tidings of their glorious and sympathetic life?"

—Rt. Rev. Phillips Brooks, D. D.

Chapter One

When the holy angels meet us,
　As we go to join their band,
Shall we know the friends that greet us,
　In the glorious spirit-land?
Shall we see the same eyes shining
　On us, as in days of yore?
Shall we feel their dear arms twining
　Fondly 'round us as before?
Shall we know each other there?

- Rev. R. Lowry.

I was many hundred miles away from home and friends, and had been very ill for many weeks. I was entirely among strangers, and my only attendant, though of a kindly disposition, knew nothing whatever of the duties of the sick room; hence I had none of the many delicate attentions that keep up an invalid's failing strength. I had taken no nourishment of any kind for nearly three weeks, scarcely even water, and was greatly reduced in both flesh and strength, and consciousness seemed at times to wholly desert me. I had an unutterable longing for the presence of my dear distant ones; for the gentle touch of beloved hands, and whispered words of love and courage; but they never came—they could not. Responsible duties, that I felt must not be neglected, kept these dear ones much of the time in distant scenes, and I would not recall them.

I lay in a large, comfortable room, on the second floor of a house in Kentville. The bed stood in a recess at one end of the apartment, and from this recess a large stained-glass window opened upon a veranda fronting on the street. During much of my illness I lay with my face to this window, and my back to the room; and I remember thinking how easy it would be to pass through the window to the veranda, if one so desired. When the longing for the loved distant faces and voices became more than I could bear, I prayed that the dear Christ would help me to realize his blessed presence; and that since the beloved ones of earth could not minister to me, I might feel the influence of the other dear ones who are "all ministering spirits." Especially did I ask to be sustained should I indeed be called to pass through the dark waters alone. It was no idle prayer, and the response came swiftly, speedily. All anxieties and cares slipped away from me, as a worn-out garment, and peace, Christ's peace, enfolded me. I was willing to wait God's time for the coming of those so dear to me, and said to myself, more than once, "If not here, it will be there; there is no fear of disappointment there." In those wonderful days of agonized suffering, and great peace, I felt that I had truly found, as never before, the refuge of "the Everlasting Arms." They lifted me; they upbore me;

they enfolded me; and I rested in them, as a tired child upon its mother's bosom. One morning, dark and cold and stormy, after a day and night of intense suffering, I seemed to be standing on the floor by the bed, in front of the stained-glass window. Some one was standing by me, and, when I looked up, I saw it was my husband's favorite brother, who "Crossed the flood" many years ago.

"My dear brother Frank!" I cried out joyously, "how good of you to come!"

"It was a great joy to me that I could do so, little sister," he said gently. "Shall we go now?" and he drew me toward the window.

I turned my head and looked back into the room that somehow I felt I was about to leave forever. It was in its usual good order: a cheery, pretty room. The attendant sat by the stove at the farther end, comfortably reading a newspaper; and on the bed, turned toward the window, lay a white, still form, with the shadow of a smile on the poor, worn face. My brother drew me gently, and I yielded, passing with him through the window, out on the veranda, and from thence, in some unaccountable way, down to the street. There I paused and said earnestly:

"I cannot leave Will and our dear boy."

"They are not here, dear, but hundreds of miles away," he answered.

"Yes, I know, but they will be here. Oh, Frank, they will need me—let me stay!" I pleaded.

"Would it not be better if I brought you back a little later—after they come?" he said, with a kind smile.

"Would you surely do so?" I asked.

"Most certainly, if you desire it. You are worn out with the long suffering, and a little rest will give you new strength."

I felt that he was right, said so in a few words, and we started slowly up the street. He had drawn my hand within his arm, and endeavored to interest me, as we walked. But my heart clung to the dear ones whom I felt I was not to see again on earth, and several times I stopped and looked wistfully back the way we had come. He was very patient and gentle with me, waiting always till I was ready to proceed again; but at last my hesitation became so great that he said pleasantly:

"You are so weak I think I had better carry you;" and without waiting for a reply, he stooped and lifted me in his arms, as though I had been a little child; and, like a child, I yielded, resting my head upon his shoulder, and laying my arm about his neck. I felt so safe, so content, to be thus in his care. It seemed so sweet, after the long, lonely struggle, to have some one assume the responsibility of caring thus tenderly for me.

He walked on with firm, swift steps, and I think I must have slept; for the next I knew, I was sitting in a sheltered nook, made by flowering shrubs, upon the softest and most beautiful turf of grass, thickly studded with fragrant flowers, many of them the flowers I had known and loved on earth. I remember noticing heliotrope, violets, lilies of the valley, and mignonette, with many others of like nature wholly unfamiliar to me. But even in that first moment I observed how perfect in its way was every plant and flower. For instance, the heliotrope, which with us often runs into long, ragged sprays, there grew upon short, smooth stems, and each leaf was perfect and smooth and glossy, instead of being rough and coarse-looking; and the flowers peeped up from the deep grass, so like velvet, with sweet, happy faces, as though inviting the admiration one could not withhold.

And what a scene was that on which I looked as I rested upon this soft, fragrant cushion, secluded and yet not hidden! Away, away—far beyond the limit of my vision, I well knew—stretched this wonderful sward of perfect grass and flowers; and out of it grew equally wonderful trees, whose drooping branches were laden with exquisite blossoms and fruits of many kinds. I found myself thinking of St. John's vision in the Isle of Patmos, and "the tree of life" that grew in the midst of the garden, bearing "twelve manner of fruits, and whose leaves were for the healing of the nations." Beneath the trees, in many happy groups, were little children, laughing and playing, running hither and thither in their joy, and catching in their tiny hands the bright-winged birds that flitted in and out among them, as though sharing in their sports, as they doubtless were. All through the grounds, older people were walking, sometimes in groups, sometimes by twos, sometimes alone, but all with an air of peacefulness and happiness that made itself felt by even me, a stranger. All were in spotless white, though many wore about them or carried in their hands clusters of beautiful flowers. As I looked upon their happy faces and their spotless robes, again I thought, "These are they who have washed their robes, and made them white in the blood of the Lamb."

Look where I would, I saw, half hidden by the trees, elegant and beautiful houses of strangely attractive architecture, that I felt must be the homes of the happy inhabitants of this enchanted place. I caught glimpses of sparkling fountains in many directions, and close to my retreat flowed a river, with placid breast and water clear as crystal. The walks that ran in many directions through the grounds appeared to me to be, and I afterward found were, of pearl, spotless and pure, bordered on either side by narrow streams of pellucid water, running over stones of gold. The one thought that fastened itself upon me as I looked, breathless and speechless, upon this scene, was "Purity, purity!" No shadow of dust; no taint of decay on fruit or flower; everything perfect, everything pure. The grass and flowers looked as though fresh-washed by summer showers, and not a single blade was any color but the brightest green. The air was soft and balmy, though invigorating; and instead of sunlight there was a golden and rosy glory everywhere; something like the afterglow of a Southern sunset in midsummer.

As I drew in my breath with a short, quick gasp of delight, I heard my brother, who was standing beside me, say softly, "Well?" and, looking up, I discovered that he was watching me with keen enjoyment. I had, in my great surprise and delight, wholly forgotten his presence. Recalled to myself by his question, I faltered:

"Oh, Frank, that I—" when such an overpowering sense of God's goodness and my own unworthiness swept over me that I dropped my face into my hands, and burst into uncontrollable and very human weeping.

"Ah!" said my brother, in a tone of self-reproach, "I am inconsiderate." And lifting me gently to my feet, he said, "Come, I want to show you the river."

When we reached the brink of the river, but a few steps distant, I found that the lovely sward ran even to the water's edge, and in some places I saw the flowers blooming placidly down in the depths, among the many-colored pebbles with which the entire bed of the river was lined.

"I want you to see these beautiful stones," said my brother, stepping into the water and urging me to do the same.

I drew back timidly, saying, "I fear it is cold."

"Not in the least," he said, with a reassuring smile. "Come."

"Just as I am?" I said, glancing down at my lovely robe, which, to my great joy, I found was similar to those of the dwellers in that happy place.

"Just as you are," with another reassuring smile.

Thus encouraged, I, too, stepped into the "gently flowing river," and to my great surprise found the water, in both temperature and density, almost identical with the air. Deeper and deeper grew the stream as we passed on, until I felt the soft, sweet ripples playing about my throat. As I stopped, my brother said, "A little farther still."

"It will go over my head," I expostulated.

"Well, and what then?"

"I cannot breathe under the water—I will suffocate."

An amused twinkle came into his eyes, though he said soberly enough, "We do not do those things here."

I realized the absurdity of my position, and with a happy laugh said, "All right; come on," and plunged headlong into the bright water, which soon bubbled and rippled several feet above my head. To my surprise and delight, I found I could not only breathe, but laugh and talk, see and hear, as naturally under the water as above it. I sat down in the midst of the many-colored pebbles, and filled my hands with them, as a child would have done. My brother lay down upon them, as he would have done on the green sward, and laughed and talked joyously with me.

"Do this," he said, rubbing his hands over his face, and running his fingers through his dark hair.

I did as he told me, and the sensation was delightful. I threw back my loose sleeves and rubbed my arms, then my throat, and again thrust my fingers through my long, loose hair, thinking at the time what a tangle it would be in when I left the water. Then the thought came, as we at last arose to return, "What are we to do for towels?" for the earth-thoughts still clung to me; and I wondered, too, if the lovely robe was not entirely spoiled. But behold, as we

8

neared the shore and my head once more emerged from the water, the moment the air struck my face and hair I realized that I would need no towel or brush. My flesh, my hair, and even my beautiful garments, were soft and dry as before the water touched them. The material out of which my robe was fashioned was unlike anything that I had ever seen. It was soft and light and shone with a faint luster, reminding me more of silk crepe than anything I could recall, only infinitely more beautiful. It fell about me in soft, graceful folds, which the water seemed to have rendered even more lustrous than before.

"What marvelous water! What wonderful air!" I said to my brother, as we again stepped upon the flowery sward "Are all the rivers here like this one?"

"Not just the same, but similar," he replied.

We walked on a few steps, and then I turned and looked back at the shining river flowing on tranquilly. "Frank, what has that water done for me?" I said. "I feel as though I could fly."

He looked at me with earnest, tender eyes, as he answered gently, "It has washed away the last of the earth-life, and fitted you for the new life upon which you have entered."

"It is divine!" I whispered,

"Yes, it is divine," he said.

Chapter Two

O City of Peace! in thy palaces fair
   Loved faces and forms we can see;
And sweet voices float to us thro' the calm air
   That whisper, "We're watching for thee!"

We walked on for some distance in silence, my heart wrestling with the thoughts of the new, strange life, my eyes drinking in fresh beauty at every step. The houses, as we approached and passed them, seemed wondrously beautiful to me. They were built of the finest marbles, encircled by broad verandas, the roofs or domes supported by massive or delicate pillars or columns; and winding steps led down to the pearl and golden walks. The style of the architecture was unlike anything I had ever seen, and the flowers and vines that grew luxuriantly everywhere surpassed in beauty even those of my brightest dreams. Happy faces looked out from these columned walls, and happy voices rang upon the clear air, from many a celestial home.

"Frank, where are we going?" at length I asked.

"Home, little sister," he answered tenderly.

"Home? Have we a home, my brother? Is it anything like these?" I asked, with a wild desire in my heart to cry out for joy.

"Come and see," was his only answer, as he turned into a side path leading toward an exquisitely beautiful house whose columns of very light gray marble shone through the green of the overhanging trees with most inviting beauty. Before I could join him, I heard a well-remembered voice saying close beside me:

"I just had to be the first to bid you welcome!" and looking around, I saw the dearly-beloved face of my old-time friend, Mrs. Wickham.

"Oh! Oh!" I cried, as we met in a warm embrace.

"You will forgive me, Col. Sprague," she said a moment later, giving her hand cordially to my brother. "It seems unpardonable to intercept you thus, in almost the first hour, but I heard that she was coming, and I could not wait. But now that I have looked upon her face, and heard her dear voice, I will be patient till I can have her for a long, long talk."

"You must come in and see her now," said my brother cordially.

"Do, do come!" I urged.

"No, dear friends, not now. You know, dear little Blossom," (the old pet name for me years ago) "we have all eternity before us! But you will bring her to me soon, Col. Sprague?" she said.

"Just as soon as I may, dear madam," he replied, with an expressive look into her eyes.

"Yes, I understand," she said softly, with a sympathetic glance at me. Then with a warm hand-clasp, and the parting injunction, "Come very soon," she passed swiftly out of my sight.

"Blessed woman!" I said, "what a joy to meet her again!"

"Her home is not far away; you can often see her. She is indeed a lovely woman. Now, come, little sister, I long to give you welcome to our home," saying which, he took my hand and led me up the low steps on to the broad veranda, with its beautiful inlaid floor of rare and costly marbles, and its massive columns of gray, between which, vines covered with rich, glossy leaves of green were intermingled with flowers of exquisite color and delicate perfume hanging in heavy festoons. We paused a moment here, that I might see the charming view presented on every side.

"It is heavenly!" I said.

"It is heavenly," he answered. "It could not be otherwise."

I smiled my acknowledgment of this truth—my heart was too full for words.

"The entire house, both below and above, is surrounded by these broad verandas. But come within."

He led me through a doorway, between the marble columns, into a large reception hall, whose inlaid floor, mullioned window, and broad, low stairway at the far end, at once held my fancy. Before I could speak, my brother turned to me, and, taking both my hands, said:

"Welcome, a thousand welcomes, dearest sister, to your heavenly home!"

"Is this beautiful place indeed to be my home?" I asked, as well as my emotion would allow.

"Yes, dear," he replied. "I built it for you and my brother, and I assure you it has been a labor of love."

"It is your home, and I am to stay with you?" I said, a little confused.

"No, it is your home, and I am to stay with you till my brother comes."

"Always, dear brother, always!" I cried, clinging to his arm.

He smiled and said, "We will enjoy the present; we never will be far apart again. But come, I am eager to show you all."

Turning to the left, he led me, still through the beautiful marble columns that everywhere seemed substituted for doorways, into a large, oblong room, upon whose threshold I stopped in wondering delight. The entire walls and floor of the room were still of that exquisite light gray marble, polished to the greatest luster; but over walls and floors were strewn exquisite, long-stemmed roses, of every variety and color, from the deepest crimson to the most delicate shades of pink and yellow.

"Come inside," said my brother.

"I do not wish to crush those perfect flowers," I answered.

"Well, then, suppose we gather some of them."

I stooped to take one from the floor close to my feet, when lo! I found it was imbedded in the marble. I tried another with the same astonishing result, then turning to my brother, I said:

"What does it mean? You surely do not tell me that none of these are natural flowers?"

He nodded his head with a pleased smile, then said: "This room has a history. Come in and sit with me here upon this window-seat, where you can see the whole room, and let me tell you about it." I did as he desired, and he continued: "One day as I was busily working upon the house, a company of young people, boys and girls, came to the door, and asked if they might enter. I gladly gave assent, and then one of them said:

"'Is this house really for Mr. and Mrs. Sprague?'

"'It is,' I answered.

"'We used to know and love them. They are our friends, and the friends of our parents, and we want to know if we may not do something to help you make it beautiful?'

"'Indeed you may,' I said, touched by the request. 'What can you do?'

"We were here at the time, and looking about, one of them asked, 'May we beautify this room?'

"'Undoubtedly,' I said, wondering what they would try to do.

"At once the girls, all of whom had immense bunches of roses in their hands, began to throw the flowers broadcast over the floor and against the walls. Wherever they struck the walls, they, to even my surprise, remained, as though in some way permanently attached. When the roses had all been scattered, the room looked just as it does now, only the flowers were really

11

fresh-gathered roses. Then the boys each produced a small case of delicate tools, and in a moment all, boys and girls, were down upon the marble floor and busy at work. How they did it I do not know—it is one of the celestial arts, taught to those of highly artistic tastes—but they embedded each living flower just where and as it had fallen, in the marble, and preserved it as you see before you. They came several times before the work was completed, for the flowers do not wither here, nor fade, but were always fresh and perfect. And such a merry, happy company of young people, I never saw before. They laughed and chatted and sang, as they worked; and I could not help wishing more than once that the friends whom they had left mourning for them might look in upon this happy group, and see how little cause they had for sorrow. At last when all was complete, they called me to see their work, and I was not chary of my praises either for the beauty of the work or for their skill in performing it. Then, saying they would be sure to return when either of you came, they went away together, to do something of the kind elsewhere, I doubt not."

Happy tears had been dropping upon my hands, clasped idly in my lap, during much of this narrative, and now I asked half-brokenly, for I was great-ly touched:

"Who were these lovely people, Frank? Do you know them?"

"Of course, I know them now; but they were all strangers to me till they came here that first morning, except Lulu Sprague."

"Who are they?"

"There were three Marys—Mary Green, Mary Bates, Mary Chalmers; Lulu Sprague and Mae Camden. These were the girls, each lovely and beautiful. The boys, all manly, fine fellows, were Carroll Ashland, Stanley and David Chalmers."

"Precious children!" I said. "How little I thought my love for them, in the olden days, would ever bring to me this added happiness here! How little we know of the links binding the two worlds!"

"Ah, yes!" said my brother, "that is just it. How little we know! If only we could realize while we are yet mortals, that day by day we are building for eternity, how different our lives in many ways would be! Every gentle word, every generous thought, every unselfish deed, will become a pillar of eternal beauty in the life to come. We cannot be selfish and unloving in one life, and generous and loving in the next; the two lives are too closely blended—one but a continuation of the other. But come now to the library."

Rising, we crossed the room that henceforward was to hold for me such tender associations, and entered the library. It was a glorious apartment—the walls lined from ceiling to floor with rare and costly books. A large, stained-glass window opened upon the front veranda, and two large bow-windows, not far apart, were in the back of the room. A semicircular row of shelves, supported by very delicate pillars of gray marble, about six feet high, extended some fifteen feet into the spacious main room and cut it into two sections lengthwise, each with one of the bowed windows in the back, leaving still a large space beyond the dividing line, where the two sections united again into one. The concave side of the semicircle of shelves was toward the entrance of the room; and close to it, not far removed from the bowed window, stood a beautiful writing-desk, with everything ready for use; and upon it was a chaste golden bowl, filled with scarlet carnations, of whose spicy odor I had been dimly conscious for some time.

"My brother's desk," said Frank.

"And his favorite flowers," I added.

"Yes, that follows. Here we never forget the tastes and preferences of those we love."

It is not to be supposed that these details were at once noticed by me, but they unfolded to me gradually as we lingered, talking together. My first sensation upon entering the room was genuine surprise at the sight of the books, and my first words were:

"Why, have we books in heaven?"

"Why not?" asked my brother. "What strange ideas we mortals have of the pleasures and duties of this blessed life! We seem to think that death of the body means an entire change to the soul. But that is not the case, by any means. We bring to this life the same tastes, the same desires, the same knowledge, we had before death. If these were not sufficiently pure and good to form a part of this life, then we ourselves may not enter. What would be the use of our ofttimes long lives, given to the pursuit of certain worthy and legitimate knowledge, if at death it all counts as nothing, and we begin this life on a wholly different line of thought and study? No, no; would that all could understand, as I said before, that we are building for eternity during our earthly life! The purer the thoughts, the nobler the ambitions, the loftier the aspirations, the higher the rank we take among the hosts of heaven; the more earnestly we follow the studies and duties in our life of probation, the better fitted we shall be to carry them forward, on and on to completion and perfection here."

"But the books—who writes them? Are any of them books we knew and loved below?"

"Undoubtedly, many of them; all, indeed, that in any way helped to elevate the human mind or immortal soul. Then, many of the rarest minds in the earth-life, upon entering on this higher life, gain such elevated and extended views of the subjects that have been with them lifelong studies, that, pursuing them with zest, they write out for the benefit of those less gifted, the higher, stronger views they have themselves acquired, thus remaining leaders and teachers in this rarer life, as they were while yet in the world. Is it to be expected that the great soul who has so recently joined our ranks, whose 'Changed Life' and 'Pax Vobiscum' uplifted so many lives while on earth, should lay his pen aside when his clear brain and great heart have read the mystery of the higher knowledge? Not so. When he has conned his lessons

13

well, he will write them out for the benefit of others, less gifted, who must follow. Leaders there must always be, in this divine life, as in the former life—leaders and teachers in many varied lines of thought. But all this knowledge will come to you simply and naturally as you grow into the new life."

Chapter Three

When I shall meet with those that I have loved,
Clasp in my arms the dear ones long removed,
And find how faithful Thou to me hast proved,
    I shall be satisfied.

- Horatius Bonar.

After a short rest in this lovely room among the books, my brother took me through all the remaining rooms of the house; each perfect and beautiful in its way, and each distinctly and imperishably photographed upon my memory. Of only one other will I speak at this time. As he drew aside the gauzy gray draperies, lined with the most delicate shade of amber, which hung before the columned doorway of a lovely room on the second floor of the house, he said:

"Your own special place for rest and study."

The entire second story of the house, indoors, instead of being finished in gray marble, as was the first floor, was finished with inlaid woods of fine, satiny texture and rare polish; and the room we now entered was exquisite both in design and finish. It was oblong in shape, with a large bowed window at one end, similar to those in the library, a portion of which was directly beneath this room. Within this window, on one side, stood a writing desk of solid ivory, with silver appointments; and opposite was a case of well-filled bookshelves of the same material. Among the books I found afterward many of my favorite authors. Rich rugs, silver-gray in color, lay scattered over the floor, and all the hangings in the room were of the same delicate hue and texture as those at the entrance. The framework of the furniture was of ivory; the upholstering of chairs and ottomans of silver-gray cloth, with the finish of finest satin; and the pillows and covering of the dainty couch were of the same. A large bowl of wrought silver stood upon the table near the front window, filled with pink and yellow roses, whose fragrance filled the air; and several rarely graceful vases also were filled with roses. The entire apartment was beautiful beyond description; but I had seen it many times before I was fully able to comprehend its perfect completeness. Only one picture hung upon the walls, and that was a life-size portrait of the Christ, just opposite the couch. It was not an artist's conception of the human Christ, bowed under the weight of the sins of the world, nor yet the thorn-crowned head of the crucified Savior of mankind; but the likeness of the living Master, of

14

Christ the victorious, of Christ the crowned. The wonderful eyes looked directly and tenderly into your own, and the lips seemed to pronounce the benediction of peace. The ineffable beauty of the divine face seemed to illumine the room with a holy light, and I fell upon my knees and pressed my lips to the sandaled feet so truthfully portrayed upon the canvas, while my heart cried, "Master, beloved Master and Savior!" It was long before I could fix my attention on anything else; my whole being was full of adoration and thanksgiving for the great love that had guided me into this haven of rest, this wonderful home of peace and joy.

After some time spent in this delightful place, we passed through the open window on to the marble terrace. A stairway of artistically finished marble wound gracefully down from this terrace to the lawn beneath the trees, no pathway of any kind approaching at its foot—only the flowery turf. The fruit-laden branches of the trees hung within easy reach from the terrace, and I noticed as I stood there that morning seven varieties. One kind resembled our fine Bartlett pear, only much larger, and infinitely more delicious to the taste, as I soon found. Another variety was in clusters, the fruit also pear-shaped, but smaller than the former, and of a consistency and flavor similar to the finest frozen cream. A third, something like a banana in shape, they called bread-fruit; it was not unlike our dainty finger-rolls to the taste. It seemed to me at the time, and really proved to be so, that in variety and excellence, food for the most elegant repast was here provided without labor or care. My brother gathered some of the different varieties and bade me try them. I did so with much relish and refreshment. Once the rich juice from the pear-like fruit (whose distinctive name I have forgotten, if indeed I ever knew it,) ran out profusely over my hands and the front of my dress. "Oh!" I cried, "I have ruined my dress, I fear!"

My brother laughed genially, as he said, "Show me the stains."

To my amazement not a spot could I find.

"Look at your hands," he said.

I found them clean and fresh; as though just from the bath.

"What does it mean? My hands were covered with the thick juice of the fruit."

"Simply," he answered, "that no impurity can remain for an instant in this air. Nothing decays, nothing tarnishes, or in any way disfigures or mars the universal purity or beauty of the place. As fast as the fruit ripens and falls, all that is not immediately gathered at once evaporates, not even the seed remaining."

I had noticed that no fruit lay beneath the trees—this, then, was the reason for it.

"'And there shall in no wise enter into it anything that defiled!,'" I quoted thoughtfully.

"Yes, even so," he answered; "even so."

We descended the steps and again entered the "flower-room." As I stood once more admiring the inlaid roses, my brother asked:

"Whom, of all the friends you have in heaven, do you most wish to see?"

"My father and mother," I answered quickly.

He smiled so significantly that I hastily turned, and there, advancing up the long room to meet me, I saw my dear father and mother, and with them my youngest sister. With a cry of joy, I flew into my father's outstretched arms, and heard, with a thrill of joy, his dear, familiar "My precious little daughter!"

"At last! at last!" I cried, clinging to him. "At last I have you again!"

"At last!" he echoed, with a deep-drawn breath of joy. Then he resigned me to my dear mother, and we were soon clasped in each other's embrace.

"My precious mother!" "My dear, dear child!" we cried simultaneously; and my sister enfolding us both in her arms, exclaimed with a happy laugh, "I can not wait! I will not be left outside!" and disengaging one arm, I threw it about her into the happy circle of our united love.

Oh, what an hour was that! I did not dream that even heaven could hold such joy. After a time my brother, who had shared our joy, said:

"Now, I can safely leave you for a few hours to this blessed reunion, for I have other work before me."

"Yes," said my father, "you must go. We will with joy take charge of our dear child."

"Then for a brief while good-by," said my brother kindly. "Do not forget that rest, especially to one but recently entered upon the new life, is not only one of the pleasures, but one of the duties of heaven."

"Yes, we will see that she does not forget that," said my father, with a kindly smile and glance.

Chapter Four

O joys that are gone, will you ever return
   To gladden our hearts as of yore?
Will we find you awaiting us, some happy morn,
   When we drift to Eternity's shore?
Will dear eyes meet our own, as in days that are past?
   Will we thrill at the touch of a hand?
O joys that are gone, will we find you at last
   On the shores of that wonderful land?

Soon after my brother's departure my mother said, grasping my hand:

"Come, I am eager to have you in our own home;" and we all passed out of the rear entrance, walked a few hundred yards across the soft turf, and entered a lovely home, somewhat similar to our own, yet still unlike it in many details. It also was built of marble, but darker than that of my brother's home. Every room spoke of modest refinement and cultivated taste, and the home air about it was at once delightfully perceptible. My father's study was on the second floor, and the first thing I noticed on entering was the luxuriant branches and flowers of an old-fashioned hundred-leafed rose tree, that covered the window by his desk.

"Ah!" I cried, "I can almost imagine myself in your old study at home, when I look at that window."

"Is it not a reminder?" he said, laughing happily. "I almost think sometimes it is the same dear old bush, transplanted here."

"And it is still your favorite flower?" I queried.

He nodded his head, and said, smiling:

"I see you remember still the childhood days." And he patted my cheek as I gathered a rose and fastened it upon his breast.

"It seems to me this ought to be your home, dear; it is our father's home," said my sister wistfully.

"Nay," my father quickly interposed. "Col. Sprague is her legitimate guardian and instructor. It is a wise and admirable arrangement. He is in every way the most suitable instructor she could possibly have. Our Father never errs."

"Is not my brother's a lovely character?" I asked.

"Lovely indeed; and he stands very near to the Master. Few have a clearer knowledge of the Divine Will, hence few are better fitted for instructors. But I, too, have duties that call me for a time away. How blessed to know there can never again be long separations! You will have two homes now, dear child—your own and ours."

"Yes, yes!" I said. "I shall be here, I suspect, almost as much as there."

At this moment a swift messenger approached my father and spoke a few low words.

"Yes, I shall go at once," he replied, and, waving his hand in adieu, departed with the angelic guide.

"Where do my father's duties mostly lie?" I asked my mother.

"He is called usually to those who enter life with little preparation—that which on earth we call death-bed repentance. You know what wonderful success he always had in winning souls to Christ; and these poor spirits need to be taught from the very beginning. They enter the spirit-life in its lowest phase, and it is your father's pleasant duty to lead them upward step by step. He is devoted to his work and greatly beloved by those he thus helps. He often allows me to accompany him and labor with him, and that is such a pleasure to me! And do you know"—with an indescribable look of happiness—"I forget nothing now!"

It had been her great burden, for some years before her death, that memory failed her sadly, and I could understand and sympathize with her present delight.

"Dear heart!" I cried, folding my arms tenderly about her, "then it is like the early years of your married life again?"

"Precisely," she answered joyously.

A little later my sister drew me tenderly aside and whispered, "Tell me of my boy, of my precious son. I often see him; but we are not permitted to know as much always of the earthly life as we once believed we should. The Father's tender wisdom metes out to us the knowledge he sees is best, and we are content to wait his time for more. All you can tell would not be denied me. Is he surely, surely coming to me sometime? Shall I hold him again in my arms, my darling boy?"

"I am sure—yes, I am sure you will. Your memory is very precious to him."

Then I told her all I could recall of the son with whom she had parted while he was but a child—now grown to man's estate, honored and loved, with home and wife and son to comfort and bless him.

"Then I can wait," she said, "if he is sure to come to me at last, when his earthly work is done, bringing his wife and son. How I shall love them, too!"

At this moment I felt myself encircled by tender arms, and a hand was gently laid on my eyes.

"Who is it?" some one whispered softly.

"Oh, I know the voice, the touch!—dearest, dearest Nell!" I cried, and, turning quickly, threw my arms about the neck of my only brother.

He gathered me a moment warmly to his heart, then in his old-time playful way lifted me quite off my feet in his strong arms, saying:

"She has not grown an inch; and is not, I believe, a day older than when we last parted! Is she, Joe?" turning to our sister.

"It does not seem so," said my sister, "but I thought she would never come."

"Trust her for that!" he said. "But come, now; they have had you long enough for the first visit; the rest of us want you for awhile. Come with us, Jodie. Mother, I may have them both for a little time, may I not? or will you come, too?" turning to our mother with a caressing touch.

"I cannot go, dear boy; I must be here when your father returns. Take your sisters; it is a blessed sight to see you all again together."

"Come then," he said; and, each taking one of my hands, we went out together.

"Halt!" he suddenly called, in his old-time military fashion, after a short walk, and we stopped abruptly in front of a dainty house built of the finest polished woods. It was beautiful both in architecture and finish.

"How lovely!" I cried; and with a bow of charming humility he said:

"The home of your humble servant. Enter."

I paused a moment on the wide veranda to examine a vine, wreathed about the graceful columns of highly-polished wood, and my brother laughingly said to my sister:

"She is the same old Sis! We will not get much good out of her until she has learned the name of every flower, vine and plant in heaven."

"Yes, you will," I said, shaking my head at his happy face, "but I mean to

18

utilize you whenever I can; I have so much to learn."

"So you shall, dear," he answered gently. "But come in."

Stepping inside a lovely vestibule, out of which opened, from every side, spacious rooms, he called softly "Alma!" At once from one of these, a fair woman approached us.

"My dear child!" I said, "it does not seem possible! You were but a child when I last saw you."

"She is still her father's girl," said my brother, with a fond look. "She and Carrie, whom you never saw, make a blessed home for me. Where is your sister, daughter?"

"She is at the great music-hall. She has a very rich voice that she is cultivating," Alma said, turning to me. "We were going to find our aunt when she returned," she added.

"True, true," said my brother; "but come."

Then they showed me the lovely home, perfect and charming in every detail. When we came out upon a side veranda, I saw we were so near an adjoining house that we could easily step from one veranda to the other.

"There!" said my brother, lightly lifting me over the intervening space. "There is some one here you will wish to see." Before I could question him, he led me through the columned doorway, saying, "People in heaven are never 'not at home' to their friends."

The house we entered was almost identical in construction and finish with that of my brother Nell, and, as we entered, three persons came eagerly forward to greet me.

"Dear Aunt Gray!" I cried. "My dear Mary—my dear Martin! What a joy to meet you again!"

"And here," said my aunt reverently.

"Yes, here," I answered in like tone.

It was my father's sister, always a favorite aunt, with her son and his wife. How we did talk and cling to one another, and ask and answer questions!

"Pallas is also here, and Will, but they have gone with Carrie to the music hall," said Martin.

"Martin, can you sing here?" I asked. He always was trying to sing on earth, but could not master a tune.

"A little," he answered, with his old genial laugh and shrug; "we can do almost anything here that we really try to do."

"You should hear him now, cousin, when he tries to sing," said his wife, with a little touch of pride in her voice. "You would not know it was Martin. But is it not nice to have Dr. Nell so near us? We are almost one household, you see. All felt that we must be together."

"It is indeed," I answered, "although you no longer need him in his professional capacity."

"No, thanks to the Father; but we need him quite as much in many other ways."

"I rather think I am the one to be grateful," said my brother. "But, sister, I promised Frank that you should go to your own room awhile; he thought it wise that you should be alone for a time. Shall we go now?"

"I am ready," I answered, "though these delightful reunions leave no desire for rest."

"How blessed," said my aunt, "that there is no limit here to our mutual enjoyment! We have nothing to dread, nothing to fear. We know at parting that we shall meet again. We shall often see each other, my child."

Then my brother went with me to my own home, and, with a loving embrace, left me at the door of my room.

Once within, I lay down upon my couch to think over the events of this wonderful day; but, looking upward at the divine face above me, I forgot all else, and, Christ's peace enfolding me like a mantle, I became "as one whom his mother comforteth." While I lay in this blissful rest, my brother Frank returned, and, without rousing me, bore me in his strong arms again to earth. I did not know, when he left us in our home, upon what mission he was going, though my father knew it was to return to my dear husband and accompany him upon his sad journey to his dead wife; to comfort and sustain and strengthen him in those first lonely hours of sorrow. They deemed it best, for wise reasons, that I should wait awhile before returning, and taste the blessedness of the new life, thus gaining strength for the trial before me.

Chapter Five

Are they not all ministering spirits, sent forth to minister for them who shall be heirs of salvation? - **Heb. 1: 14.**

How oft do they their silver bowers leave,
  To come to succor us that succor want!
How oft do they with golden pinions cleave
  The flitting skyes, like flying pursuivant,
Against fowle feendes to ayd us militant!
  They for us fight, they watch, and dewly ward,
And their bright squadrons round about us plant.
  And all for love, and nothing for reward;
O why should heavenly God to men have such regard!

- Edmund Spenser.

When I aroused from my sleep it was in the gray light of earth's morning, and I was standing on the doorstep of the house in Kentville that my brother and I had left together, some thirty-six hours before, reckoned by earth-time. I shuddered a little with a strange chill when I saw where we were, and turned quickly to my brother Frank, who stood beside me. He put his arm about me, and with a reassuring smile, said:

"For their sakes be brave and strong, and try to make them understand your blessed change."

I did not try to answer, though I took heart, and entered with him into the house. Everything was very quiet—no one seemed astir. My brother softly opened a door immediately to the right of the entrance, and motioned me to enter. I did so, and he closed it behind me, remaining himself outside.

Something stood in the center of the room, and I soon discovered that it was a pall. It was a great relief to me to see that it was not black, but a soft shade of gray. Someone was kneeling beside it, and as I slowly approached I saw it was my dear son. He was kneeling upon one knee, with his elbow resting on the other knee, and his face buried in his hand. One arm was thrown across the casket, as though he were taking a last embrace of his "little mother." I saw that the form within the casket lay as though peacefully sleeping, and was clad in silver gray, with soft white folds about the neck and breast. I was grateful that they had remembered my wishes so well.

I put my arms about the neck of my darling son, and drew his head gently against my breast, resting my cheek upon his bowed head. Then I whispered, "Dearest, I am here beside you—living, breathing, strong and well. Will you not turn to me, instead of to that lifeless form in the casket? It is only the worn-out tenement—I am your living mother."

He lifted his head as though listening; then, laying his hand tenderly against the white face in the casket he whispered, "Poor, dear little mother!" and again dropped his face into both hands, while his form shook with convulsive sobs.

As I strove to comfort him, the door opened and his lovely girl-wife entered. I turned to meet her as she came slowly towards us. Midway in the room we met, and, taking both her hands tenderly in mine, I whispered, "Comfort him, darling girl, as only you can; he needs human love."

She paused a moment irresolutely, looking directly into my eyes, then passed on and knelt beside him, laying her upturned face against his shoulder. I saw his arm steal around her and draw her closely to him, then I passed from the room, feeling comforted that they were together.

Outside the door I paused an instant, then, slowly ascending the stairs, I entered the once familiar room, whose door was standing ajar. All remained as when I had left it, save that no still form lay upon the white bed. As I expected, I found my precious husband in this room. He sat near the bay window, his arm resting upon the table, and his eyes bent sorrowfully upon the floor. My heart's best friend sat near him and seemed trying to comfort him. When I entered the room our brother Frank arose from a chair close beside him and passed out, with a sympathetic look at me. I went at once to my dear husband, put my arms about him, and whispered:

"Darling! darling, I am here!"

He stirred restlessly without changing his position. Virginia said, as though continuing a conversation, "I am sure she would say you left nothing undone that could possibly be done for her."

"She is right," I whispered.

"Still she was alone at the last," he moaned.

"Yes, dear, but who could know it was the last? She sank so suddenly under the pain. What can I say to comfort you? Oh, Will, come home with us! She would want you to, I am sure."

He shook his head sadly, while the tears were in his eyes, as he said: "Work is my only salvation. I must go back in a very few days."

She said no more, and he leaned back wearily in his easy-chair. I crept more closely to him and suddenly his arms closed about me. I whispered, "There, dear, do you not see that I am really with you?"

He was very still, and the room was very quiet but for the ticking of my little clock still standing upon the dressing-case. Presently I knew by his regular breathing that he had found a short respite from his sorrow. I slipped gently from his arms and went to my friend, kneeling beside her, and folding my arms about her.

"Virginia, Virginia! You know I am not dead! Why do you grieve?"

She looked over at the worn face of the man before her, then dropped her face into her hand, whispering, as though she had heard me and would answer:

"Oh, Bertha darling, how could you leave him?"

"I am here, dearest! Do realize that I am here!"

She did not heed me, but sat absorbed in sorrowful thought.

A few minutes later a stranger entered the room, and in a low voice said something about its being "near train time," and brought my husband his hat. He arose and gave his arm to Virginia, and, our son and his wife meeting them at the door, they started to descend the stairs. Just then my husband paused and cast one sorrowful glance around the room, his face white with pain. Our dear daughter stepped quickly to him, and, placing both arms about his neck, drew his face down to hers. ("God bless her in all things!" I softly prayed.) An instant they stood thus, then stifling his emotion, they all passed down the stairs into the room I had first entered.

I kept very close to my dear husband, and never for a single instant left him through all the solemn and impressive services; through the sad journey to our old home; the last rites at the grave; the after-meeting with friends; and his final return to the weary routine of labor. How thankful I was that I had been permitted to taste, during that wonderful day in heaven, the joys of the blessed life! How else could I ever have passed calmly through those trying scenes, and witnessed the sorrow of those so dear to my heart? I recognize the wisdom and mercy of the Father in having so ordered it.

I soon found that my husband was right; work was his great refuge. During the day the routine of labor kept brain and hands busy, leaving the heart but little opportunity to indulge its sorrow. Night was his trying time. Kind friends would stay with him till bedtime; after that he was alone. He would turn restlessly on his pillow, and often arise and go into the adjoining room that had formerly been mine, and gaze upon the vacant bed with tearful eyes. It took all my powers to in any degree soothe and quiet him. After a time my brother Frank and I arranged to spend alternate nights with him, that he might never be alone, and especially were we with him upon his journeys. We found to our great joy that our influence over him was hourly growing stronger, and we were able to guide and help him in many ways.

One night as I was silently watching beside him while he slept, many months after he was alone, I became conscious that evil threatened him. He was sleeping very peacefully, and I knew his dreams were happy ones by the smile upon his dear face. I passed into the hall of the hotel where he was staying, and found it dense with smoke. I hastened back to him and called, and tried to shake him, but he slept on peacefully. Then I called with all my strength, "Will!" close to his ear.

Instantly he started up and said, "Yes, dear, I am coming!" just as he used to do when I called at night. Then in a moment he sank back with a sigh upon his pillow, murmuring, "What a vivid dream! I never heard her voice more distinctly in life."

"Will!" I again called, pulling him by the hand with all my strength, "rise quickly! Your life is in danger!"

In an instant he was out of bed, upon his feet, and hurriedly drawing on his clothes. "I am sure I cannot tell why I am doing this," he muttered to himself. "I only feel that I must! That surely was her voice I heard."

"Hurry! Hurry!" I urged.

He opened the door and met, not only the smoke, but tongues of flame.

"Do not try the stairway—come!" and I drew him past the stairway, and through a narrow entrance to a second hall beyond, and down a second flight of stairs, filled with smoke, but as yet no flame. Another flight still below these, then into the open air, where he staggered, faint and exhausted, on to the sidewalk, and was quickly helped by friends into a place of safety.

"I am sure I cannot tell what wakened me," he afterward said to a friend. "I dreamed I heard my wife calling me, and before I knew it I was dressing myself."

"You did hear her, I have no doubt," she said. "Are they not 'all ministering spirits, sent forth to do service for the sake of them that shall inherit salvation'? What lovelier service could she do than to thus save the life of one so dear to her, whose earth-work was not yet done? Yes, you did hear her call you in time to escape. Thank God for such ministrations."

"Yes, it must be so," he answered, with a happy look. "Thank God indeed."

After this he yielded much more readily to our influence, and thus began to enjoy, while yet upon earth, the reunion that so surely awaited us in the blessed life. I often went also to the home of our dear children, but there was so much to make them happy that they did not need me as their father did. Sometimes in hours of great physical prostration, especially during the absence of his wife, I found that I could quiet the overwrought nerves of my dear son, and lead his tired mind to restful thoughts; but with youth and strength and love to support him, the time had not yet come when my ministrations were essential.

Chapter Six

Many friends that traveled with me
   Reached Heaven's portal long ago;
One by one they left me battling
   With the dark and crafty foe.
They are watching at the portal,
   They are waiting at the door;
Waiting only for my coming—
   The beloved ones gone before.

- Mrs. H. M. Reasoner.

The first time I returned to the dear heavenly home after my long delay on earth, as I approached the entrance, in the company of my brother Frank, we saw a tall young man standing close by the open gate, looking wistfully the way we came. As we drew near, he said in an almost pathetic voice:

"Is my mother coming?"

A closer scrutiny revealed his identity, and I exclaimed with joy, extending both hands to him, "My dear Carroll!"

He smiled a bright welcome as he extended his hands, but said wistfully, "I so hoped my mother would return with you, aunt, when you came back. Did you see her?"

"Once only, for a brief moment. She is very happy and bears her years well. She will come to you now before long, but then you know it will be forever."

"Yes, I know," he answered brightly. "I will be patient. But," he added confidentially, "I so want her to see the lovely home I myself am building for her. Will you come and see it?"

"Of course I will, gladly."

"Now?"

"Yes, if I may"; looking at my brother for his sanction.

He nodded his head pleasantly as he said: "That is right, Carroll. Have her help you in every way you can. I will leave you two together, and you will bring her to me later?"

"Indeed, yes," said my nephew; and we went away happily together.

"Where is this wonderful house, Carroll?"

"Not very far beyond Mrs. Wickham's," he said.

We soon reached it, and I was truly charmed with it in every way. It was fashioned much like my brother Nell's home, and was, like it, built of pol-

24

ished woods. It was only partly finished, and was most artistically done. Although uncompleted, I was struck with the fact that everything was perfect so far as finished. There was no debris anywhere; no chips, no shavings, no dust. The wood seemed to have been perfectly prepared elsewhere—where, I have no idea. The pieces were made to fit accurately, like the parts of a great puzzle. It required much skill and artistic taste to properly adjust each to its place. This, my nephew, who even in the earthly life was quite a mechanical genius, seemed to have no difficulty in doing, and the house was slowly growing into beauty and symmetry. After showing me all over the house, he at last drew aside the hangings before an entrance, beyond which were two rooms, not only entirely finished, but beautifully furnished as well.

"I finished and furnished these rooms complete, so that if mother came before the house was ready, she could occupy them at once. You know there is no noise from workmen here; no hammering, no unwelcome sounds."

I thought at once of the Temple of Jerusalem, where, during its erection, there was "neither hammer, nor axe, nor any tool of iron heard in the house."

"It is very beautiful, my dear boy," I said enthusiastically. "It will give her great joy to know you did it for her. But what is this—a fireplace?" pausing before a lovely open chimney, wherein wood was piled ready to be lighted. "Is it ever cold enough here for fires?"

"It is never cold," he answered, "but the fire here never sends out unneeded warmth. We have its cheer and beauty and glow, without any of its discomforts. You remember my mother loves to sit by an open fire; so I have arranged this for her."

"It is charming! But you did not make the stained-glass windows also?"

"No, I have a friend who has been taught that art, and we exchange work. He helps me with the windows, and I in turn help him with his fine woodwork and inlaying. I am going to make a 'flower room' for my mother similar to yours, only of lilies and violets, which will retain their perfume always."

"How lovely! I want to thank you, dear Carroll, for your share in our 'flower room.' It is the most exquisite work I ever saw; and it is doubly so when I remember whose hands fashioned it."

"It was a labor of love with us all," he said simply.

"That is what enhances its beauty for me," I said. "But sit here by me now, and tell me about yourself. Do you spend all your time at this delightful work?"

"Oh, no, indeed! Perhaps what we used to call two or three hours daily. Much of my time is still spent with my Grandfather R——. I do not know what I should have done when I first came here, but for him. I was so ignorant about this life, and came so suddenly."

"Yes, dear boy, I know," I said sympathetically.

"He met me at the very entrance, and took me at once home, where he and grandma did everything possible to instruct and help me. But I was, I am still, far below what I ought to be. I would give a year out of this blessed life—I

25

would even go back to the old life for an entire year—if I only could go to my old friends, or better, into every Sunday-school in the world, and beseech the girls and boys to try to understand and profit by the instruction there received. Why, I used to go to Sunday-school, Sunday after Sunday, help sing the hymns, and read the lesson, and listen to all that was said; and I really enjoyed every moment of the time. Sometimes I would feel a great longing after a better life, but there seemed to be no one to especially guide or help me, and, the greater part of the time, what I heard one Sunday was never once spoken of or even thought of till another Sunday came, so that the impression made was very transient. Why do not boys and girls talk more together about what they hear at Sunday-school? We were all ready enough to talk about a show of any kind, after it was over, but seldom of the Sunday-school, when together socially. Why do not teachers take more interest in the daily lives of their scholars? Why is there so little really helpful talk in ordinary home life? Oh, I wish I could go back and tell them this!"

His face beamed with enthusiasm as he talked, and I, too, wished it might be possible for him to do as he desired. But alas! "they will not be persuaded even if one arise from the dead," I thought.

"It is now time for me to go with my grandfather," he said, rising, "but we will walk together as far as your home; and you will let me often see you, will you not?"

"Gladly," I answered, as we set forth.

We still conversed of many things, as we walked, and when we parted at the door I said, "I am soon to learn how to weave lovely draperies; then I can help you, when you are ready for them."

"That will make my work more delightful still," was his reply, as he hastened on in the direction of my father's home.

Chapter Seven

She is not dead—the child of our affection—
    But gone unto that school
Where she no longer needs our poor protection,
    And Christ himself doth rule.
Day after day we think what she is doing
    In those bright realms of air;
Year after year, her tender steps pursuing,
    Behold her grown more fair.

                                                    - Longfellow.

Hark! 'tis the voice of angels
    Borne in a song to me,
Over the fields of glory,
    Over the jasper sea!

                                                    - W. H. Doane.

As time passed, and I grew more accustomed to the heavenly life around me, I found its loveliness unfolded to me like the slow opening of a rare flower. Delightful surprises met me at every turn. Now a dear friend, from whom I had parted years ago in the earth-life, would come unexpectedly upon me with cordial greeting; now one—perhaps on earth greatly admired, but from whom I had held aloof, from the fear of unwelcome intrusion—would approach me, showing the lovely soul so full of responsive kindness and congenial thought, that I could but feel a pang of regret for what I had lost. Then the clear revelation of some truth, only partly understood in life, though eagerly sought for, would stand out clear and strong before me, overwhelming me with its lustre, and perhaps showing the close tie linking the earth-life with the divine. But the most wonderful to me was the occasional meeting with some one whom I had never hoped to meet "over there," who, with eager handclasp and tearful eyes, would pour forth his earnest thanks for some helpful word, some solemn warning, or even some stern rebuke, that had turned him, all unknown to myself, from the paths of sin into the "life everlasting." Oh, the joy to me of such a revelation! Oh, the regret that my earth-life had not been more full of such work for eternity!

My first impulse daily on arousing from happy, blissful rest, was to hasten to the "river of life" and plunge into its wonderful waters, so refreshing, so invigorating, so inspiring. With a heart full of thanksgiving and lips full of joyful praise, morning after morning, sometimes in company with my brother, sometimes alone, I hastened thither, returning always full of new life and hope and purpose to our home, where for a time each day I listened to the entrancing revelations and instructions of my brother. One morning, soon after my return from my first visit to earth, as I was on the way to the river, my voice joined to the wonderful anthem of praise everywhere sounding, I saw a lovely young girl approaching me swiftly, with outstretched arms.

"Dear, dear Aunt Bertha!" she called, as she drew near, "do you not know me?"

"My little Mae!" I cried, gathering the dainty creature into my arms. "Where did you spring from so suddenly, dear? Let me look at you again!" holding her a moment at arm's length, only to draw her again tenderly to me.

"You have grown very beautiful, my child. I may say this to you here without fear, I am sure. You were always lovely; you are simply radiant now. Is it this divine life?"

"Yes," she said modestly and sweetly; "but most of all the being near the Savior so much."

"Ah, yes, that is it—the being near Him! That will make any being radiant and beautiful," I said.

"He is so good to me; so generous, so tender! He seems to forget how little I have done to deserve his care."

"He knows you love him, dear heart; that means everything to him."

"Love him! Oh, if loving him deserves reward, I am sure I ought to have every wish of my heart, for I love him a thousandfold better than anything in earth or heaven. I would die for him!"

The sweet face grew surpassingly radiant and beautiful as she talked, and I began to dimly understand the wonderful power of Christ among the redeemed in heaven. This dear child, so lovely in all mortal graces, so full of earth's keenest enjoyments during the whole of her brief life—pure and good, as we count goodness below, yet seemingly too absorbed in life's gayeties to think deeply of the things she yet in her heart revered and honored, now in this blessed life counted the privilege of loving Christ, of being near him, beyond every other joy! And how that love refined and beautified the giver! As a great earthly love always shines through the face and elevates the whole character of the one who loves, so this divine love uplifts and glorifies the giver, until not only the face but the entire person radiates the glory that fills the heart.

"Come with me to the river, Mae," I said presently, after we had talked together for some time; "come with me for a delightful plunge."

"Gladly," she said; "but have you ever been to the lake or the sea?"

"The lake or the sea?" I echoed. "No indeed. Are there a lake and sea here?"

"Certainly there are," said Mae, with a little pardonable pride that she should know more of the heavenly surroundings than I. "Shall we go to the lake to-day, and leave the sea for another day? Which shall it be?"

"Let it be the lake to-day," I said.

So, turning in an entirely different direction from the path that led to the river, we walked joyously on, still talking as we went. So much to ask, so much to recall, so much to look forward to with joy!

Once she turned to me and asked quickly:

"When is my Uncle Will coming?"

My hand closed tightly over hers, and a sob almost rose in my throat, though I answered calmly:

"That is in God's hands alone; we may not question."

"Yes, I know. His will is always right; but I so long to see my dear uncle again; and to 'long' is not to repine."

She had grown so womanly, so wise, this child of tender years, since we parted, that it was a joy to talk with her. I told her of my sad errand to earth, and the sorrow of the dear ones I had left.

"Yes, yes, I know it all!" she whispered, with her soft arms about me. "But it will not be long to wait. They will come soon. It never seems long to wait for anything here. There is always so much to keep one busy; so many pleasant duties, so many joys—oh, it will not be long!"

Thus she cheered and comforted me as we walked through the ever-varying and always perfect landscape. At length she cried, lifting her arm and pointing with her rosy finger:

"Behold! Is it not divinely beautiful?"

I caught my breath, then stopped abruptly and covered my face with my hands to shield my eyes from the glorified scene. No wonder my brother had not sooner brought me to this place; I was scarcely yet spiritually strong enough to look upon it. When I again slowly lifted my head, Mae was standing like one entranced. The golden morning light rested upon her face, and, mingling with the radiance that had birth within, almost transfigured her. Even she, so long an inhabitant here, had not yet grown accustomed to its glory.

"Look, darling auntie! It is God's will that you should see," she softly whispered, not once turning her eyes away from the scene before her. "He let me be the one to show you the glory of this place!"

I turned and looked, like one but half awakened. Before us spread a lake as smooth as glass, but flooded with a golden glory caught from the heavens, that made it like a sea of molten gold. The blossom- and fruit-bearing trees grew down to its very border in many places, and far, far away, across its shining waters, arose the domes and spires of what seemed to be a mighty city. Many people were resting upon its flowery banks, and on the surface of the water were boats of wonderful structure, filled with happy souls, and propelled by an unseen power. Little children, as well as grown persons, were floating upon or swimming in the water; and as we looked a band of singing cherubs, floating high overhead, drifted across the lake, their baby voices borne to us where we stood, in notes of joyful praise.

"Come," said Mae, seizing my hand, "let us join them"; and we hastened onward.

"Glory and honor!" sang the child voices. "Dominion and power!" caught up and answered the voices of the vast multitude together, and in the strain I found that Mae and I were joining. The cherub band floated onward, and away in the distance we caught the faint melody of their sweet voices, and the stronger cadence of the response from those waiting below.

We stood upon the margin of the lake, and my cheeks were tear-bedewed and my eyes dim with emotion. I felt weak as a little child; but oh, what rapture, what joy unspeakable filled and overmastered me! Was I dreaming? Or was this indeed but another phase of the immortal life?

Mae slipped her arm about my neck and whispered, "Dearest, come. After the rapture—rest."

I yielded to her passively; I could not do otherwise. She led me into the water, down, down into its crystal depths, and when it seemed to me we must be hundreds of feet beneath the surface, she threw herself prostrate and bade me do the same. I did so, and immediately we began to slowly rise. Presently I found that we no longer rose, but were slowly floating in mid-current, many feet still beneath the surface. Then appeared to me a marvel. Look where I would, perfect prismatic rays surrounded me. I seemed to be resting in the heart of a prism; and such vivid yet delicate coloring, mortal eyes never rested upon. Instead of the seven colors, as we see them here, the colors blended in such rare graduation of shades as to make the rays seem almost infinite, or they really were so; I could not decide which.

As I lay watching this marvelous panorama, for the colors deepened and faded like the lights of the aurora borealis, I was attracted by the sound of distant music. Although Mae and I no longer clung together, we did not drift apart, as one would naturally suppose we might, but lay within easy speaking-distance of each other, although few words were spoken by either of us; the silence seemed too sacred to be lightly broken. We lay upon, or rather within, the water, as upon the softest couch. It required no effort whatever to keep ourselves afloat; the gentle undulation of the waves soothed and rested us. When the distant music arrested my attention, I turned and looked at Mae. She smiled back at me, but did not speak. Presently I caught the words, "Glory and honor, dominion and power," and I knew it was still the cherub choir, although they must now be many miles distant. Then the soft tones of a bell—a silver bell with silver tongue—fell on my ear, and as the last notes died away, I whispered:

"Tell me, Mae."

"Yes, dear, I will. The waters of this lake catch the light in a most marvelous manner, as you have seen; a wiser head than mine must tell you why. They also transmit musical sounds—only musical sounds—for a great distance. The song was evidently from the distant shore of the lake."

"And the bell?"

"That is the bell which in the city across the lake calls to certain duties at this hour."

"There never was a sweeter call to duty," I said.

"Yes, its notes are beautiful. Hark! now it rings a chime."

We lay and listened, and as we listened a sweet spell wrapped me round, and I slept as peacefully as a child on its mother's bosom. I awoke with a strange sense of invigoration and strength. It was a feeling wholly dissimilar to that experienced during a bath in the river, yet I could not explain how. Mae said:

"One takes away the last of the earth-life, and prepares us for the life upon which we enter; the other fills us to overflowing with a draught from the Celestial Life itself."

And I think the child was right.

When we emerged from the water we found the banks of the lake almost deserted, every one having gone, at the call of the bell, to the happy duties of the hour. Groups of children still played around in joyous freedom. Some climbed the trees that overhung the water, with the agility of squirrels, and dropped with happy shouts of laughter into the lake, floating around upon its surface like immense and beautiful water-lilies or lotus flowers.

"No fear of harm or danger; no dread of ill, or anxiety lest a mishap occur; security, security and joy and peace! This is indeed the blessed life," I said, as we stood watching the sports of the happy children.

"I often think how we were taught to believe that heaven was where we would wear crowns of gold and stand with harps always in our hands! Our crowns of gold are the halos His blessed presence casts about us; and we do not need harps to accentuate our songs of praise. We do see the crowns, and we do hear the angelic harps, when and as God wills it, but our best worship is to do his blessed will," said Mae as we turned to go.

"You are wise in the lore of heaven, my child," I answered; "how happy I am to learn from one so dear! Tell me all about your life here."

So as we walked she told me the history of her years in heaven her duties, her joys, her friends, her home—with all the old-time freedom. I found her home was distant from our own—far beyond the spires of the great city across the lake—but she added:

"What is distance in heaven? We come and go at will. We feel no fatigue, no haste, experience no delays; it is blessed, blessed!"

Not far from our home we saw a group of children playing upon the grass, and in their midst was a beautiful great dog, over which they were rolling and tumbling with the greatest freedom. As we approached he broke away from them and came bounding to meet us, and crouched and fawned at my very feet with every gesture of glad welcome.

"Do you not know him, auntie?" Mae asked brightly.

"It is dear old Sport!" I cried, stooping and placing my arms about his neck, and resting my head on his silken hair. "Dear old fellow! How happy I am to have you here!"

He responded to my caresses with every expression of delight, and Mae laughed aloud at our mutual joy.

"I have often wondered if I should not some day find him here. He surely deserves a happy life for his faithfulness and devotion in the other life. His intelligence and his fidelity were far above those of many human beings whom we count immortal."

"Hark! 'tis the voice of angels
"Hark! 'tis the voice of angels
"Hark! 'tis the voice of angels
Born in a song to me,
Over the fields of glory,
Over the jasper sea!"

"Did he not sacrifice his life for little Will?"

"Yes; he attempted to cross the track in front of an approaching train, because he saw it would pass between him and his little master, and feared he was in danger. It cost his life. He always placed himself between any of us and threatened danger, but Will he seemed to consider his especial charge. He was a gallant fellow—he deserves immortality. Dear, dear old Sport, you shall never leave me again!" I said, caressing him fondly.

31

At this he sprang to his feet, barking joyously, and gambolled and frolicked before us the rest of the way home, then lay down upon the doorstep, with an upward glance and a wag of his bushy tail, as though to say, "See how I take you at your word!"

"He understands every word we say," said Mae.

"Of course he does; he only lacks speech to make him perfect. I somehow hoped he might find it here."

"He would not be half so interesting if he could talk," said Mae.

"Possibly not. How silken and beautiful his long hair is!"

"He has his bath in the river every day, and it leaves its mark on him also. Do you know I think one of the sweetest proofs we have of the Father's loving care for us is, that we so often find in this life the things which gave us great happiness below. The more unexpected this is, the greater joy it brings. I remember once seeing a beautiful little girl enter heaven, the very first to come of a large and affectionate family. I afterward learned that the sorrowful cry of her mother was, 'Oh, if only we had someone there to meet her, to care for her!' She came, lovingly nestled in the Master's own arms, and a little later, as he sat, still caressing and talking to her, a remarkably fine Angora kitten, of which the child had been very fond, and which had sickened and died some weeks before, to her great sorrow, came running across the grass and sprang directly into her arms, where it lay contentedly. Such a glad cry as she recognized her little favorite, such a hugging and kissing as that kitten received, made joy even in heaven! Who but our loving Father would have thought of such comfort for a little child? She had evidently been a timid child; but now as the children gathered about her, with the delightful freedom they always manifest in the presence of the beloved Master, she, looking up confidingly into the tender eyes above her, began to shyly tell of the marvelous intelligence of her dumb pet, until at last Jesus left her contentedly playing among the flowers with the little companions who had gathered about her. Our Father never forgets us, but provides pleasures and comforts for us all, according to our individual needs."

"When shall I behold the Savior? When shall I meet, face to face, him whom my soul so loveth?" my hungry heart began to cry out in its depths.

Mae, as though understanding the silent cry, placed both arms about my neck, looked tenderly into my eyes, and whispered:

"You, too, dearest, will see him soon. He never delays when the time is ripe for his coming. It will not be long; you, too, will see him soon."

So we parted, each to the duties of the hour.

Chapter Eight

Sae little noo I ken o' blessed, bonnie place,
I only ken it's Hame, whaur we shall see His face
It wad surely be eneuch forever mair to be
In the glory o' His presence, in oor ain countrie.
Like a bairn to his mither, a wee birdie to its nest,
I wad fain be gangin' noo unto my Savior's breast,
For he gathers in his bosom witless, worthless lambs like me,
And carries them himsel' to his ain countrie.

- Mary Lee Demarest

The following morning my brother said to me, after an interesting hour of instruction:

"Shall we go for the promised visit to Mrs. Wickham now?"

"Indeed, yes!" I answered eagerly; so we at once set forth.

We soon reached her lovely home and found her waiting at the entrance as though expecting us. After a cordial greeting to our friend, my brother said:

"I will leave you together for that 'long talk' for which I know you are both eager, and will go my way to other duties. I will find you, later on, at home." The last remark to me.

"All right," I answered. "I am familiar with the way now, and need no attendance."

After he had gone, my friend took me all over her lovely home, showing me, with great pleasure, the rooms prepared for each beloved member of her earthly household still to come. One very large room, into whose open windows at each end the blossom- and fruit-laden boughs of the immortal trees looked invitingly, was evidently her especial care; she whispered to me, "Douglass always did like a large room. I am sure he will like this one." And I was also sure.

Returning down the broad stairway, we found it entered into a very large music-room, with broad galleries supported by marble columns, running across three sides of it, on a level with the second floor. In this gallery was a number of musical instruments—harps, viols, and some unlike any instruments I had ever seen elsewhere. The room itself was filled with easy-chairs, couches and window-seats, where listeners could rest and hear the sweet harmonies from the galleries.

"My daughter," my friend explained, "who left us in early childhood, has received a fine musical training here, and is fond of gathering in her young friends and giving us quite often a musical treat. You know our old home of Springville has furnished some rare voices for the heavenly choirs. Mary Allis, Will Griggs, and many others you will often hear in this room, I trust."

We re-entered, from this room, the dainty reception hall opening upon the front veranda and outer steps. Here Mrs. Wickham drew me to a seat beside her and said:

"Now, tell me everything of the dear home and all its blessed inmates."

Holding each other's hands as we talked, she questioning, I answering, things too sacred to be repeated here were dwelt upon for hours. At last she said, rising hastily:

"I will leave you for a little while—nay, you must not go," as I would have risen, "there is much yet to be said; wait here, I will return."

I had already learned not to question the judgment of these wiser friends, and yielded to her will. As she passed through the doorway to the inner house, I saw a stranger at the front entrance and arose to meet him. He was tall and commanding in form, with a face of ineffable sweetness and beauty. Where had I seen him before? Surely, surely I had met him since I came. "Ah, now I know!" I thought; "it is St. John, the beloved disciple." He had been pointed out to me one morning by the river-side.

"Peace be unto this house," was his salutation as he entered.

How his voice stirred and thrilled me! No wonder the Master loved him, with that voice and that face!

"Enter. Thou art a welcome guest. Enter, and I will call the mistress," I said, as I approached to bid him welcome.

"Nay, call her not. She knows that I am here; she will return," he said. "Sit thou awhile beside me," he continued, as he saw that I still stood, after I had seen him seated. He arose and led me to a seat near him, and like a child I did as I was bidden; still watching, always watching, the wonderful face before me.

"You have but lately come?" he said.

"Yes, I am here but a short time. So short that I know not how to reckon time as you count it here," I answered.

"Ah, that matters little," he said with a gentle smile. "Many cling always to the old reckoning and the earth-language. It is a link between the two lives; we would not have it otherwise. How does the change impress you? How do you find life here?"

"Ah," I said, "if they could only know! I never fully understood till now the meaning of that sublime passage, 'Eye hath not seen, nor ear heard, neither have entered into the heart of man, the things which God hath prepared for them that love him.' It is indeed past human conception." I spoke with deep feeling.

"'For them that love him'? Do you believe that all Christians truly love him?" he asked. "Do you think they love the Father for the gift of the Son and the Son because of the Father's love and mercy? Or is their worship ofttimes that of duty rather than love?" He spoke reflectively and gently.

"Oh," I said, "you who so well know the beloved Master—who were so loved by him—how can you doubt the love he must inspire in all hearts who seek to know him?"

34

A radiant glow overspread the wonderful face, which he lifted, looking directly at me—the mist rolled away from before my eyes—and I knew him! With a low cry of joy and adoration, I threw myself at his feet, bathing them with happy tears. He gently stroked my bowed head for a moment, then rising, lifted me to his side.

"My Savior—my King!" I whispered, clinging closely to him.

"Yes, and Elder Brother and Friend," he added, wiping away tenderly the tears stealing from beneath my closed eyelids.

"Yes, yes, 'the chiefest among ten thousand, and the One altogether lovely!'" again I whispered.

"Ah, now you begin to meet the conditions of the new life! Like many another, the changing of faith to sight with you has engendered a little shrinking, a little fear. That is all wrong. Have you forgotten the promise, 'I go to prepare a place for you; that where I am, there ye may be also'? If you loved me when you could not see me except by faith, love me more now when we have really become 'co-heirs of the Father.' Come to me with all that perplexes or gladdens; come to the Elder Brother always waiting to receive you with joy."

Then he drew me to a seat, and conversed with me long and earnestly, unfolding many of the mysteries of the divine life. I hung upon his words; I drank in every tone of his voice; I watched eagerly every line of the beloved face; and I was exalted, uplifted, upborne, beyond the power of words to express. At length with a divine smile, he arose.

"We will often meet," he said; and I, bending over, pressed my lips reverently to the hand still clasping my own. Then laying his hands a moment in blessing upon my bowed head, he passed noiselessly and swiftly from the house.

As I stood watching the Savior's fast-receding figure, passing beneath the flower-laden trees, I saw two beautiful young girls approaching the way he went. With arms intertwining they came, happily conversing together, sweet Mary Bates and Mae Camden. When they saw the Master, with a glad cry they flew to meet him, and as he joyously extended a hand to each, they turned, and each clinging to his hand, one upon either side, accompanied him on his way, looking up trustingly into his face as he talked with them, and apparently conversing with him with happy freedom. I saw his face from time to time in profile, as he turned and looked down lovingly, first upon one, then the other lovely upturned face, and I thought, "That is the way he would have us be with him—really as children with a beloved elder brother." I watched them till the trees hid them from my sight, longing to gather the dear girls to my heart, but knowing his presence was to them then more than aught else; then I turned and passed softly through the house to the beautiful entrance at the rear. Just before I reached the door I met my friend Mrs. Wickham. Before I could speak, she said:

"I know all about it. Do not try to speak; I know your heart is full. I will see you very soon—there, go!" and she pushed me gently to the door.

How my heart blessed her—for it indeed seemed sacrilege to try to talk on ordinary topics after this blessed experience. I did not follow the walk, but kept across the flowery turf, beneath the trees, till I reached home. I found my brother sitting upon the veranda, and as I ascended the steps he rose to meet me. When he looked into my face, he took both hands into his for an instant, and simply said, very gently:

"Ah, I see. You have been with the Master!" and stepped aside almost reverently for me to enter the house.

I hastened to my room, and, dropping the draperies behind me at the door, I threw myself upon the couch, and with closed eyes lived over every instant I had spent in that hallowed Presence. I recalled every word and tone of the Savior's voice, and fastened the instructions he had given me indelibly upon my memory. I seemed to have been lifted to a higher plane of existence, to have drunk deeper draughts from the fountain of all good, since I had met "Him whom my soul loved." It was a long, blessed communion that I held thus with my own soul on that hallowed day. When I looked upon the pictured face above me, I wondered that I had not at once recognized the Christ, the likeness was so perfect. But I concluded that for some wise purpose my "eyes were holden" until it was his pleasure that I should see him as he is.

When at last I arose, the soft golden twilight was about me, and I knelt by my couch, to offer my first prayer in heaven. Up to this time my life there had been a constant thanksgiving—there had seemed no room for petition. Now as I knelt all I could utter over and over, was:

"I thank Thee, blessed Father; I thank Thee, I thank Thee!"

When I at last descended the stairs, I found my brother standing in the great "flower-room," and, going to him, I said softly:

"Frank, what do you do in heaven when you want to pray?"

"We praise!" he answered.

"Then let us praise now," I said.

And standing there, with clasped hands, we lifted up our hearts and voices in a hymn of praise to God; my brother with his clear, strong voice leading, I following. As the first notes sounded, I thought the roof echoed them; but I soon found that other voices blended with ours, until the whole house seemed filled with unseen singers. Such a grand hymn of praise earth never heard. And as the hymn went on, I recognized many dear voices from the past—Will Griggs' pathetic tenor, Mary Allis' exquisite soprano, and many another voice that wakened memories of the long ago. Then as I heard sweet child-voices, and looked up, I saw above us such a cloud of radiant baby faces as flooded my heart with joy. The room seemed filled with them.

"Oh, what a life—what a divine life!" I whispered, as, after standing until the last lingering notes had died away, my brother and I returned to the veranda and sat in the golden twilight.

36

"You are only in the first pages of its record," he said. "Its blessedness must be gradually unfolded to us, or we could not, even here, bear its dazzling glory."

Then followed an hour of hallowed intercourse, when he led my soul still deeper into the mysteries of the glorious life upon which I had now entered. He taught me; I listened. Sometimes I questioned, but rarely. I was content to take of the heavenly manna as it was given me, with a heart full of gratitude and love.

Chapter Nine

Not as a child shall we again behold her;
    For when with rapture wild
In our embraces we again enfold her,
    She will not be a child,
But a fair maiden, in her Father's Mansion,
    Clothed with celestial grace,
And beautiful with all the soul's expansion
    Shall we behold her face.

- **Henry W. Longfellow**

The next day, my brother being away upon an important mission, I started out alone to see if I might not find the dear young friends of whom I had caught a fleeting glimpse the day before. I knew that all things were ordered aright in that happy world, and that sooner or later I should find them again; yet I could but hope it might be very soon. I recalled the happy light upon their fresh young faces as they had met the beloved Master, and I longed to talk with them of their life from day to day. From thinking of them, I began again to think of my blessed interview with Him, and became so absorbed in these thoughts that I was even oblivious to the beautiful world around me. Suddenly I heard some one say:

"Surely that is Mrs. Sprague!" and looking up, I saw sweet Mary Bates a few steps away, regarding me intently. I cried joyfully:

"My precious Mamie!"

She flew to me, and folding me in her arms, drew my head to her shoulder in the old caressing way, almost sobbing in her great joy.

"Dear, dear little muzzer!"—a pet name often used by her in the happy past—"how glad, how glad I am to have you here! I could scarcely wait to find you."

"How did you know I was here, Mamie?"

"The Master told me," she said softly. "Mae had already told me, and we were on the way to find you when we met him, and he told us he had just left you. Then we knew we must wait a little," she said reverently.

How my heart thrilled! He had thought about, had spoken of me, after we parted! I longed to ask her what he had said, but dared not. Seeming to divine my thoughts, she continued:

"He spoke so tenderly about you, and said we must be with you much. Mae had work to do to-day, and as she had already seen you once, I came alone. She may be here later on. May I stay a long time with you? There is so much to tell you, so much to ask about!"

"Indeed you may. I had started out to find you, when we met. Come, dear child, let us return home at once."

So, clinging to each other, we set out toward my home.

"What shall I tell you first?" I asked.

"Everything about the dear ones—every individual member of our beloved household. Begin with my precious, heart-broken mother;" here her voice broke a little, but she soon continued, "I am with her often, but her great, and I fear unreconciled, sorrow, keeps me from being the comfort to her I long to be. If only she could spend one hour with me here, could know God's wisdom and love as we know it, how the cloud would lift from her life! How she would see that the two lives, after all, are but one."

"Yes, dear," I answered, "I always urged her to think of it in that light and to trust implicitly in the Father's tender care and never-failing love; but it is difficult for us to see beyond the lonely hearthstone and the vacant chair. Still, I believe she does begin to dimly grasp the comfort you are so eager to impart."

"Ah, if only she knew that I need just that to complete my happiness now! We cannot sorrow here as we did on earth, because we have learned to know that the Will of the Father is always tender and wise; but even heaven can never be complete for me while I know that my precious mother is forgetful of her many rare blessings, simply because I may not be with her, in the flesh, to share them. There is my father, and the boys—why, I am as truly hers still as they are! I often sit with them all, with her hand in mine, or my arms about her—my dear little mother! Why must she see me, to recognize this? But this is almost complaining, is it not? Some day she will know all—we must be patient."

As we walked on slowly, conversing of the earth-life, still in many phases so dear to us, she asking eager questions, I answering as best I could, we saw a group of four persons, three women and a man, standing under the trees a little to one side of the walk. The man's back was towards us, but we at once recognized the Master. The women were all strangers, and one of them seemed to have just arrived. Her hand the Savior held, as he talked with her, while all were intently listening to his words. We regarded the group in silence as we slowly passed, not hoping for recognition from him at such a time, but just as we were opposite to them, "he turned and looked upon" us. He did not speak—but oh, that look! So full of tenderness and encouragement and benediction! It lifted us, it bore us upward, it enthralled and exalted us; and as we passed onward, the clasp of our hands tightened, and rapture unspeakable flooded our hearts.

We finished our walk in silence, and sat down on the marble steps in the shadow of the overhanging trees. The dear child nestled close against my side, and laid her head upon my shoulder, while I rested my cheek caressingly upon it. After a time I whispered, half to myself, "Was there ever such a look!"

Instantly she raised her head and looking at me, said eagerly: "You think so, too? I was sure you would. It is always just so. If he is too much engaged to speak to you at the time, he just looks at you, and it is as though he had talked a long while with you. Is he not wonderful! Why, why could we not know him on earth as we know him here?"

"How long were you here before you met him?" I asked.

"Oh, that is the wonderful part of it! His was the first face I looked upon after I left the body. I felt bewildered when I first realized that I was free, and I stood for a moment irresolute. Then I saw him standing just beside me, with that same look upon his face. At first I felt timid and half afraid. Then he stretched forth his hand to me, and said gently, 'My child, I have come to take care of you; trust me; do not be afraid.' Then I knew him, and instantly all fear left me, and I clung to him as I would have done to either of my brothers. He did not say much to me, but somehow I felt that he understood all of my thoughts. After a moment, I asked:

"'May I not remain awhile with mamma? She is heart-broken.'

"'Yes, dear child, as long as you desire,' he answered compassionately.

"'Will you also remain?' I asked, for I already felt I could not bear to have him leave me.

"He looked much pleased, as though he divined my thought, as he answered: 'Yes, I will never leave you, till you are ready to accompany me.'

"Then I went to mamma and put my arms about her, and presently the Master, too, came and whispered words of comfort to her; but I am not sure she recognized our presence, though I fancied that she grew more calm beneath my caresses. We stayed till all was over. I never left mamma an instant, except that twice I stole to poor little Hal's sick-room when he was for a short time alone. I have always felt that he recognized my presence more than any of them, he lay so still and calm when I talked to him. He seemed to be listening. When they gathered for the last time about my casket, it seemed to me I must speak, I must show myself to them! Could they for one instant have seen my living self, standing so calmly in their midst, they would have turned forever from the lifeless clay they had embalmed and beautified for the tomb. They would have known I was not there. But they would not recognize the truth. At last I pleaded with the Master to let me show myself once to them, there. But he said, 'It is not the Father's will.'

"After that I accepted fully the Father's will, and soon thereafter he brought me here in his arms. And what a blessed life it is!"

39

I can give only a brief outline of our conversation on that first happy day. It is too sacred to be scanned by curious eyes. We talked until the golden twilight fell, and we watched the little birds nestling in the vines, and heard afar the solemnly joyous notes of the angels' choral song, and joined our voices in the hymn of praise. Later we went to my room, and lay down upon my dainty couch for rest, and the last words I heard before sinking into heaven's blissful sleep were, tenderly whispered: "Dear, dear little muzzer, I am so glad and happy that you are here!"

More than once the question has been asked, "Was there night there?" Emphatically, no! What, for want of a better designation, we may call "day," was full of a glorious radiance, a roseate golden light, which was everywhere. There is no language known to mortals that can describe this marvelous glory. It flooded the sky; it was caught up and reflected in the waters; it filled all heaven with joy and all hearts with song. After a period much longer than our longest earthly day, this glory mellowed and softened until it became a glowing twilight full of peace. The children ceased their playing beneath the trees, the little birds nestled among the vines, and all who had been busy in various ways throughout the day sought rest and quiet. But there was no darkness, no dusky shadows even—-only a restful softening of the glory.

Chapter Ten

O sweet and blessed country,
   The home of God's elect!
O sweet and blessed country
   That eager hearts expect!
There stand those halls of Zion
   All jubilant with song,
And bright with many an angel,
   And all the martyr throng.

                  - St. Bernard of Cluny.

Not long after this my brother said, "We will go to the grand auditorium this morning; it will be a rare day even here. Martin Luther is to talk on 'The Reformation; Its Causes and Effects,' and this will be supplemented by a talk from John Wesley. There may also be other speakers."

It was not the first time we had visited this great auditorium, although I have not hitherto described it. It stood upon a slight eminence, and the mighty dome was supported by massive columns of alternate amethyst and jasper. There were no walls to the vast edifice; only the great dome and supporting columns. A broad platform of precious marbles, inlaid in porphyry, arose from the center, from which the seats ascended on three sides, forming an immense amphitheater. The seats were of cedar wood highly polished; and back of the platform were heavy hangings of royal purple. An altar of solid pearl stood near the center of the platform. The great dome was deep and dark in its immensity, so that only the golden statues around its lower border were distinctly visible. All this I had noted at former visits.

When we entered, we found the building filled with people eagerly waiting for what was to follow. We soon were seated and also waiting. Soft strains of melody floated about us, from an invisible choir, and before long Martin Luther, in the prime of a vigorous manhood, ascended the steps and stood before us. It is not my purpose to dwell upon his appearance, so familiar to us all, except to say that his great intellect and spiritual strength seemed to have added to his already powerful physique, and made him a fit leader still, even in heavenly places.

His discourse would of itself fill a volume, and could not be given even in outline, in this brief sketch. He held us enthralled by the power of his will and his eloquence. When he at length retired, John Wesley took his place, and the saintly beauty of his face, intensified by the heavenly light upon it, was wonderful. His theme was "God's love;" and if in the earth-life he dwelt upon it with power, he now swept our souls with the fire of his exaltation, until we were as wax in his hands. He showed what that love had done for us, and how an eternity of thanksgiving and praise could never repay it.

Silence, save for the faint, sweet melody of the unseen choir, rested upon the vast audience for some time after he left. All seemed lost in contemplation of the theme so tenderly dwelt upon. Then the heavy curtains back of the platform parted, and a tall form, about whom all the glory of heaven seemed to center, emerged from their folds and advanced toward the middle of the platform. Instantly the vast concourse of souls arose to their feet, and burst forth as with one voice into that grand anthem in which we had so often joined on earth:

"All hail the power of Jesus' name,
  Let angels prostrate fall;
Bring forth the royal diadem,
  And crown him Lord of all."

Such a grand chorus of voices, such unity, such harmony, such volume, was never heard on earth. It rose, it swelled, it seemed to fill not only the great auditorium, but heaven itself. And still, above it all, we heard the voices of the angel choir, no longer breathing the soft, sweet melody, but bursting forth into pæans of triumphant praise. A flood of glory seemed to fill the place, and looking upward we beheld the great dome ablaze with golden light, and the angelic forms of the no longer invisible choir in its midst, with their heavenly harps and viols, and their faces only less radiant than that of Him in whose praise they sang. And he, before whom all heaven bowed in adoration, stood with uplifted face and kingly mien, the very God of earth and heaven. He was the center of all light, and a divine radiance surrounded him that was beyond compare.

As the hymn of praise and adoration ceased, all sank slowly to their knees, and every head was bowed and every face covered as the angel choir chanted again the familiar words:

"Glory be to the Father, and to the Son, and to the Holy Ghost. As it was in the beginning, is now, and ever shall be, world without end. Amen, Amen!"

Slowly the voices died away, and a holy silence fell upon us. Presently, slowly and reverently, all arose and resumed their places. No, not all. Sweet Mary Bates had accompanied us to the sanctuary, and I now noticed that she alone still knelt in our midst, with clasped hands and radiant uplifted face, her lovely eyes fixed upon the Savior, as he still stood waiting before us, with such a look of self-forgetful adoration and love as made her herself truly divine. She was so rapt I dared not disturb her; but in a moment the Master turned and met her adoring eyes with such a look of loving recognition, that with a deep sigh of satisfied desire, as he turned again, she quietly resumed her seat beside me, slipping her little hand into mine with all the confidence of a child who feels sure it is understood to the utmost.

As I looked upon the glorious form before us, clothed in all the majesty of the Godhead, my heart tremblingly asked: "Can this indeed be the Christ-man whom Pilate condemned to die an ignominious death upon the cross?" I could not accept it. It seemed impossible that any man, however vile, could be blind to the divinity so plainly revealed in him.

Then the Savior began to speak, and the sweetness of his voice was far beyond the melody of the heavenly choir. And his gracious words! Would that I could, would that I dared, transcribe them as they fell from his lips. Earth has no language by which I could convey their lofty meaning. He first touched lightly upon the earth-life, and showed so wonderfully the link of light uniting the two lives—the past with the present. Then he unfolded to us some of the earlier mysteries of the blessed life, and pointed out the joyous duties just before us.

When he ceased, we sat with bowed heads as he withdrew. Our hearts were so enfolded, our souls so uplifted, our spirits so exalted, our whole being so permeated with his divinity, that when we arose we left the place silently and reverently, each bearing away a heart filled with higher, more divine aspirations, and clearer views of the blessed life upon which we were permitted to enter.

I can touch but lightly upon these heavenly joys. There is a depth, a mystery to all that pertains to the divine life, which I dare not try to describe; I could not if I would, I would not if I could. A sacredness enfolds it all that curious eyes should not look upon. Suffice it to say, that no joy we know on earth, however rare, however sacred, can be more than the faintest shadow of the joy we there find; no dreams of rapture, here unrealized, approach the bliss of one moment, even, in that divine world. No sorrow; no pain; no sickness; no death; no partings; no disappointments; no tears but those of joy; no broken hopes; no mislaid plans; no night, nor storm, nor shadows even; but light and joy and love and peace and rest forever and forever. "Amen," and again my heart says reverently, "Amen."

Chapter Eleven

Jerusalem! Jerusalem!
  Thy streets of pearl and gold
Are trod by the blest feet of them
  We knew and loved of old.
Their voices full of calm delight
  Steal through the radiant air—
Jerusalem! Jerusalem!
  Our hearts are with them there!

As the days passed I found my desires often led me to the sacred lake, sometimes alone, sometimes with one or more of my own family circle—my revered father and precious mother, my dear brother and sister, and many beloved friends both within and without the bond of consanguinity. It was always to me an inspiration and an uplifting. I never could grow sufficiently familiar with it to overcome the first great awe with which it inspired me; but I found that the oftener I bathed or floated and slept in its pellucid current, the stronger I grew in spirit, and the more clearly I comprehended the mysteries of the world about me. My almost daily intercourse with the dear ones of our home life from whom I had so long been separated, served to restore to me the home feeling that had been the greatest solace of my mortal life; and I began to realize that this was indeed the true life, instead of that probationary life which we had always regarded as such. I think it was the day after my return from my first visit to earth, that, as I had started to cross the sward lying between my father's house and our own, I heard my name called in affectionate tones. I turned and saw approaching me a tall, fine-looking man, whose uncovered head was silvery white, and whose deep blue eyes looked happily and tenderly into mine, as he drew near.

"Oliver!" I cried with outstretched hands of welcome, "dear, dear Oliver!" It was the husband of my eldest sister, always dearly loved.

"I did not know that you had come, until a few moments since, when our father told me. It is delightful to have you here; it seems more like the old life to see you than any of the others who are here—we were together so much during the last years of my stay," he said, grasping my hands warmly. "Where are you going now? Can you not come with me awhile? I was thinking only a few days ago how much I wished you could be here a little while before Lu came; you know her tastes so well. And now here you are! So often our unspoken wishes are thus gratified in heaven!"

"Is my sister coming soon?" I asked a little later.

"That I cannot confidently say; but you know the years of the earth-life are passing, and her coming cannot be much longer delayed. Can you come with me now?"

"Gladly," I said, turning to walk with him.

"It is only a little way from here," he said. "Just where the river bends. Lu loves the water so, I chose that spot in preference to one even nearer your home."

"This is truly enchanting!" I cried, as we drew near the place. "I have not been this way before."

"I want you to see the river from her room windows," he said; "I know you will enjoy it."

We entered the truly beautiful house, built of the purest white granite, so embedded in the foliage of the flower-laden trees that from some points only glimpses of its fine proportions could be seen.

"She loves flowers so much—will she not enjoy these trees?" he asked with almost boyish delight.

"Beyond everything," I answered.

We passed through several delightful rooms on the lower floor, and, ascending the stairway, which in itself was a dream of beauty, entered the room he was so anxious I should see. I stopped upon the threshold with an exclamation of delight, while he stood watching with keen enjoyment the expression on my face.

"It is the most delightful room I ever saw!" I cried enthusiastically.

The framework of couches, chairs and desk was of pure and spotless pearl, upholstered in dim gold; soft rugs and draperies everywhere; and through the low window, opening upon the flower-wreathed balcony, so enchanting a view of the broad, smooth river below, that again I caught my breath in delight. A thousand exquisite tints from the heavens above were reflected upon the tranquil waters, and a boat floating on the current was perfectly mirrored in the opaline-tinted ripples. Far across the shining waters the celestial hills arose, with domes and pillared temples and sparkling fountains perceptible everywhere. When at last I turned from this entrancing view, I saw on the opposite wall, smiling down upon me, the same Divine face that I daily looked upon in my own room at home.

We descended the stairs without a word, then I could only falter:

"Only heaven could give such perfection in everything!"

Oliver pressed my hand sympathetically, and let me depart without a word.

Many months, by earthly time, had passed since that day, and many times I had visited that lovely home and held sweet converse with one I loved so well. I could suggest nothing that would add to the beauty of the place, but we talked of it together, and planned for and anticipated the joy of her coming.

One day I found him absent, and though I waited long for his return, he came not. I had not seen him for several days, and concluded he had been sent upon some mission by the Master. As I passed onward to our home, I met a group of happy young girls and boys, of different ages, hastening the way I had come, with their arms full of most beautiful flowers. As they drew near I saw they were the grandchildren of my dear sister—Stanley and Mary and David and Lee and little Ruth. As soon as they saw me, they all with one accord began to shout joyfully:

"Grandma is coming! Grandma is coming! We are taking flowers to scatter everywhere! We are so glad!"

"How do you know she is coming, children? I have just been to the house—no one is there!"

"But she is coming," said little Lee. "We had a message from grandpa, and he is to bring her."

"Then I will tell the others, and we will all come to welcome her," I said.

With a great joy in my heart I hastened onward to my father's house. I found them awaiting me, full of joyful expectation.

"Yes, we also have had word," my father said, "and were only awaiting your return, that we might go together."

"Then I will go for brother Frank, that he also may accompany us," I said.

"He is here!" said a genial voice; and, looking up, I saw him at the door.

"Col. Sprague is always present when he is needed," said my father cordially.

So we set forth, a goodly company, to welcome this dearly loved one to her home—my father, my mother, and my sister Jodie; my brother the doctor, and his two fair daughters; my Aunt Gray, her son Martin, and his wife and daughter; my brother Frank and I.

As we approached the house we heard the sound of joyous voices, and looking in, we saw my sister standing in the room, her husband's arm about her, and the happy grandchildren thronged around them, like humming-birds among the flowers. But what was this? Could this radiant creature, with smooth brow and happy eyes, be the pale, wan woman I had last seen, so bowed with suffering and sorrow? I looked with eager eyes. Yes, it was my sister; but as she was full thirty years ago, with the bloom of health upon her face, and the light of youth in her tender eyes. I drew back into the shadow of the vines and let the others precede me, for my heart was full of a strange, triumphant joy. This truly was the "victory over death" so surely promised by our risen Lord. I watched the happy greetings, and the way she took each beloved one into her tender arms. When, one by one, she had greeted and embraced them all, I saw her, with a strange yearning at my heart, turn and look wistfully around, then whisper to my father:

"Is not my little sister here?"

I could wait no longer, but, hastening to her side, cried:

"Dearest, I am here! Welcome! Welcome!"

She folded me to her heart and held me fast in her warm arms, she showered me with kisses upon my upturned face, while I returned each loving caress, and laughed and cried for very gladness that she had come at last. Oh, what a family reunion was that inside the walls of heaven! And how its bliss was heightened by the sure knowledge (not the hope) that there should be no partings for us henceforth forever!

My brother Oliver looked on with proud and happy eyes. The hour for which he had longed and waited had come to him at last; his home-life would now be complete for evermore. I told him how I had waited for him that day, and he said, "We saw you as you left the house, but were too distant to call you. I had taken her into the river, and she had looked at and admired the house very greatly before she knew it was our home."

"What did she do when she saw her lovely room?"

"Cried like a child, and clung to me, and said, 'This more than repays us for the lost home of earth!' If the children had not come, I think she would have been at that window still!" he said, laughing happily.

"I am glad you had her all to yourself at the first," I whispered; "you deserved that happiness, dear, if any man ever did."

He smiled gratefully, and looked over at his wife, where she stood the center of a happy group.

"Does she not look very young to you, Oliver?" I asked.

"The years rolled from her like a mask, as we sat beneath the water in the river. Ah, truly in those life-giving waters we do all 'renew our youth'; but she became at once uncommonly fair and young."

"Her coming has brought youth likewise to you," I said, noting his fresh complexion and his sparkling eyes; "but I hope it will not change your silver hair, for that is to you a crown of glory."

He looked at me a moment critically, then said:

"I wonder if you realize the change that has likewise come to you in this wonderful clime?"

"I?" I said, a little startled at the thought; "I confess I have not once thought of my personal appearance. I realize what, through the Father's mercy, this life has done for me spiritually, but as for the other, I have never given it an instant's thought."

"The change is fully as great in your case as in Lu's, though with you the change has been more gradual," he said.

I felt a strange thrill of joy that when my dear husband should come to me, he would find me with the freshness and comeliness of our earlier years. It was a sweet thought, and my heart was full of gratitude to the Father for this further evidence of his loving care. So we talked together as the hours sped, until my father said:

"Come, children; we must not forget that this dear daughter of mine needs rest this first day in her new home. Let us leave her and her happy husband to their new-found bliss."

So with light hearts we went our way, and left them to spend their first hours in heaven together.

Chapter Twelve

Holy, holy, holy! All the saints adore Thee,
Casting down their golden crowns around the glassy sea;
Cherubim and Seraphim falling down before Thee,
Which wert, and art, and evermore shalt be.

- Bishop Heber.

After we had left my parents and friends on our return from our welcome to my sister, my brother hastened away upon some mission, and I walked on alone toward the sacred lake. I felt the need of a rest in its soothing waters after the exciting scenes through which I had passed. I had hitherto visited the lake in the early morning hours; it was now something past noontide of the heavenly day, and but few persons lingered on the shore. The boats that sped across its calm surface seemed to be filled rather with those intent upon some duty than simply pleasure-seekers. I walked slowly down into the water, and soon found myself floating, as at former times, in midcurrent. The wonderful prismatic rays that in the early morning were such a marvel, now blended into a golden glory, with different shades of rose and purple flashing athwart their splendor. To me it seemed even more beautiful than the rainbow tints; just as the maturer joys of our earthly life cast into shadow, somewhat, the more evanescent pleasures of youth. I could but wonder what its evening glories would be, and resolved to come at some glowing twilight, and see if they would not remind me of the calm hours of life's closing day. I heard the chimes from the silver bell of the great city ringing an anthem as I lay, and its notes seemed to chant clearly:

"Holy! Holy! Holy! Lord God Almighty!" The waters took up the song and a thousand waves about me responded, "Holy! Holy! Holy!"

The notes seemed to "vibrate," if I may use the expression, upon the waves, producing a wondrously harmonious effect. The front row in the battalion of advancing waves softly chanted "Holy" as they passed onward; immediately the second roll of waves took up the word that the first seemed to have dropped as it echoed the second "Holy" in the divine chorus, then it, too, passed onward to take up the second note as the third advancing column caught the first; and so it passed and echoed from wave to wave, until it seemed millions of tiny waves about me had taken up and were bearing their part in this grand crescendo—this wonderful anthem. Language fails me—I cannot hope to convey to others this experience as it came to me. It was grand, wonderful, overpowering. I lay and listened until my whole being was filled with the divine melody, and I seemed to be a part of the great chorus, then I, too, lifted up my voice and joined with full heart in the thrilling song of praise.

I found that, contrary to my usual custom, I floated rapidly away from the shore whence I had entered the water, and after a time was conscious that I was approaching a portion of the lake shore I had never yet visited. Refreshed and invigorated, I ascended the sloping banks, to find myself in the midst of a lovely suburban village, similar to the one where our own home was situated. There was some difference in the architecture or construction of the houses, though they were no less beautiful than others I had seen. Many were constructed of polished woods, and somewhat resembled the finest of the chalets one sees in Switzerland, though far surpassing them in all that gives pleasure to the artistic eye.

As I wandered on, feasting my eyes upon the lovely views about me, I was particularly pleased by the appearance of an unusually attractive house. Its broad verandas almost overhung the waters of the lake, the wide low steps running on one side of the house quite to the water's edge. Several graceful swans were leisurely drifting about with the current, and a bird similar to our Southern mocking-bird, but with softer voice, was singing and swinging in the low branches overhead. There were many larger and more imposing villas near, but none possessed for me the charm of this sweet home.

Beneath one of the large flowering trees close by this cottage home, I saw a woman sitting, weaving with her delicate hands, apparently without shuttle or needle, a snow-white gossamer-like fabric that fell in a soft fleecy heap at her side as the work progressed. She was so very small in stature that at first glance I supposed she was a child; but a closer scrutiny showed her to be a mature woman, though with the glow of youth still upon her smooth cheek. Something familiar in her gestures, rather than her appearance, caused me to feel that it was not the first time we had met; and growing accustomed now to the delightful surprises that met me everywhere in this world of rare delights, I drew near to accost her, when, before I could speak, she looked up, and the doubt was gone.

"Maggie!" "Mrs. Sprague dear!" we cried simultaneously, as, dropping her work from her hands, she stepped quickly up to greet me.

Our greeting was warm and fervent, and her sweet face glowed with a welcome that reminded me of the happy days when we had met, in the years long gone, by the shore of that other beautiful lake in the world of our earthlife.

"Now I know why I came this way to-day—to find you, dear," I said, as we sat side by side, talking as we never had talked on earth; for the sweet shyness of her mortal life had melted away in the balmy air of heaven.

"What is this lovely fabric you are weaving?" I presently asked, lifting the silken fleecy web in my fingers as I spoke.

"Some draperies for Nellie's room," she said. "You know we two have lived alone together so much, I thought it would seem more like home to her, to us

48

both, if we did the same here. So this cottage is our own special home, just a step from Marie's," pointing to an imposing house a few yards distant, "and I am fitting it up as daintily as I can, especially her room."

"Oh, let me help you, Maggie dear!" I said. "It would be such a pleasure to me."

She hesitated an instant, with something of the old-time shyness, then said:

"That is so like you, dear Mrs. Sprague. I have set my heart on doing Nellie's room entirely myself—there is no hurry about it, you know—but if you really would enjoy it, I shall love to have you help me in the other rooms."

"And will you teach me how to weave these delicate hangings?"

"Yes, indeed. Shall I give you your first lesson now?"

Lifting the dainty thread, she showed me how to toss and wind it through my fingers till it fell away in shining folds. It was very light and fascinating work, and I soon was weaving it almost as rapidly as she did.

"Now, I can help Carroll!" was my happy thought, as I saw the shimmering fabric grow beneath my hands. "To-morrow I will go and show him how beautifully we can drape the doors and windows."

So in heaven our first thought ever is to give pleasure to others.

"You are an apt scholar," said Maggie, laughing happily; "and what a charming hour you have given me!"

"What a charming hour you have given me, my dear!" I answered.

When we parted it was with the understanding that every little while I was to repeat the visit. When I urged her likewise to come to me, the old-time shyness again appeared, as she said:

"Oh, they are all strangers to me, and here we shall be entirely alone. You come to me."

So I yielded, as in heaven we never seek to gain reluctant consent for any pleasure, however dear; and many were the happy hours spent with her in the cottage by the lake.

Chapter Thirteen

"I take these little lambs," said He
    And lay them in my breast;
Protection they shall find in Me,
    In Me be ever blest."

- Samuel Stennett.

On one of my walks about this time, I chanced upon a scene that brought to mind what Mae had said to me about the Savior's love for little children. I found him sitting beneath one of the flowering trees upon the lake shore, with about a dozen children of all ages clustered around him. One dainty little tot, not more than a year old, was nestled in his arms, with her sunny

49

head resting confidingly upon his bosom, her tiny hands filled with the lovely water-lilies that floated everywhere on the waters. She was too young to realize how great her privilege was, but seemed to be enjoying his care to the utmost. The others sat at his feet, or leaned upon his knees; and one dear little fellow, with earnest eyes, stood by him, leaning upon his shoulder, while the Master's right arm encircled him. Every eye was fixed eagerly upon Jesus, and each child appeared alert to catch every word he said. He seemed to be telling them some very absorbing story, adapted to their childish tastes and capacities. I sat down upon the sward among a group of people, a little removed from the children, and tried to hear what he was saying, but we were too far away to catch more than a sentence now and then, and in heaven one never intrudes upon another's privileges or pleasures. So we simply enjoyed the smiles and eager questions and exclamations of the children, and gathered a little of the tenor of the story from the disjointed sentences which floated to us.

"A little child lost in the dark woods of the lower world—" we heard the Master say, in response to the inquiring looks of the interested children.

"Lions and bears—" came later on.

"Where was his papa?" asked an anxious voice.

We could not hear the reply, but soon a little fellow leaning upon the Savior's knee, said confidently: "No lions and bears up here!"

"No," he replied, "nothing to harm or frighten my little children here!"

Then as the story deepened and grew in interest, and the children pressed more closely about the Master, he turned with a sweet smile—and we could see an increased pressure of the encircling arm—to the little fellow with the earnest eyes who leaned upon his shoulder, and said:

"What, Leslie, would you have done, then?"

With a bright light in his eyes and a flush on his fair cheek, the child answered quickly and emphatically:

"I should have prayed to Thee and asked Thee to 'close the lion's mouth,' as Thou didst for Daniel, and Thou wouldst have done it!"

"Ah," I thought, "could C—— and H—— see the look the beloved Master cast upon their boy as he made his brave reply, they would be comforted even for the absence of their darling."

Lost in these thoughts, I heard no more that passed, until an ecstatic shout from the little folks proclaimed how satisfactorily the story had ended, and, looking up, I saw the Savior passing onward, with the baby still in his arms, and the children trooping about him.

"Of such is the kingdom of heaven." How well he understood! How much he loved them!

I, too, arose and started homeward. I had not gone far before I met my brother Frank, who greeted me with:

"I am on my way to the city by the lake; will you accompany me?"

"It has been long my wish to visit the city. I only waited until you thought it wise for me to go," I answered.

"You are growing so fast in the knowledge of the heavenly ways," he said, "that I think I might venture to take you almost anywhere with me now. You acquire the knowledge for the very love of it; not because you feel it your duty to know what we would have you learn. Your eagerness to gather to yourself all truth, and at the same time your patient submission in waiting, ofttimes when I know the trial is great, have won for you much praise and love from our dear Master, who watches eagerly the progress of us all in the divine life. I think it only right that you should know of this; we need encouragement here as well as in the earth-life, though in a different way. I tell you this by divine permission. I think it will not be long before He trusts you with a mission; but this I say of myself, not by his command."

It would be impossible for me to convey, in the language of earth, the impression these words of commendation left upon me. They were so unexpected, so unforeseen. I had gone on, as my brother said, eagerly gathering the knowledge imparted to me, with a genuine love for the study of all things pertaining to the blessed life, without a thought that I in any way deserved commendation for so doing; and now I had won the approbation of the Master himself! The happiness seemed almost more than I had strength to bear.

"My brother, my dear brother!" was all I could say, in my deep joy, stopping suddenly and looking up into his face with grateful tears.

"I am so glad for you, little sister!" he said, warmly clasping my hand. "There are, you see, rewards in heaven; it does my soul good that you have unconsciously won one of these so soon."

I would I might record in detail the precious words of wisdom that fell from his lips; I would that I might recount minutely the events of that wonderful life as it was unfolded to me day by day; but I can only say, "I may not." When I undertook to make a record of that never-to-be-forgotten time, I did not realize how many serious difficulties I would have to encounter; how often I would have to pause and consider if I might really reveal this truth or paint that scene as it appeared to me. The very heart has often been left out of some wonderful scene I was attempting to describe, because I found I dared not reveal its sacred secret. I realize painfully that the narrative, as I am forced to give it, falls infinitely short of what I hoped to make it when I began. But bear with me; it is no fancy sketch I am drawing, but the veritable life beyond, as it appeared to me when the exalted spirit rose triumphant over the impoverished flesh, made slavishly subservient through suffering.

My brother and I walked slowly back to the margin of the lake, where we stepped into a boat lying near the shore, and were at once transported to the farther shore of the lake, and landed upon a marble terrace—the entrance to the city by the lake. I never knew by what power these boats were propelled. There were no oarsmen, no engine, no sails, upon the one in which we crossed the water; but it moved steadily onward till we were safely landed at our destination. Luxuriously cushioned seats were all around it, and upon one of them lay a musical instrument, something like a violin, although it had no bow, but seemed to be played by the fingers alone. Upon another seat lay a book. I picked it up and opened it; it seemed to be a continuation of that book that has stirred and thrilled millions of hearts in the mortal life—"The Greatest Thing in the World." As I glanced through it while we journeyed, I grasped the truth that this great mind already had grappled with the mighty things of eternity and given food to immortals, even as he had to those in mortal life in the years gone by.

I was roused from my thoughts by the boat touching the marble terrace, and found my brother already standing waiting to assist me to the shore. Passing up a slight acclivity, we found ourselves in a broad street that led into the heart of the city. The streets I found were all very broad and smooth, and paved with marble and precious stones of every kind. Though they were thronged with people intent on various duties, not an atom of debris, or even dust, was visible anywhere. There seemed to be vast business houses of many kinds, though I saw nothing resembling our large mercantile establishments. There were many colleges and schools; many book and music-stores and publishing houses; several large manufactories, where, I learned, were spun the fine silken threads of manifold colors which were so extensively used in the weaving of the draperies I have already mentioned. There were art rooms, picture galleries and libraries, and many lecture halls and vast auditoriums. But I saw no churches of any kind. At first this somewhat confused me, until I remembered that there are no creeds in heaven, but that all worship together in harmony and love—the children of one and the same loving Father. "Ah," I thought, "what a pity that that fact, if no other in the great economy of heaven, could not be proclaimed to the inhabitants of earth! How it would do away with the petty contentions, jealousies and rivalries of the church militant! No creeds in heaven! No controverted points of doctrine! No charges of heresy brought by one professed Christian against another! No building up of one denomination upon the ruins or downfall of a different sect! But one great universal brotherhood whose head is Christ, and whose corner-stone is Love." I thought of the day we had listened in the great auditorium at home to the divine address of our beloved Master; of the bowed heads and uplifted voices of that vast multitude as every voice joined in the glorious anthem, "Crown Him Lord of All!" and I could have wept to think of the faces that must some day be bowed in shame when they remember how often they have in mortal life said to a brother Christian, "Stand aside; I am holier than thou!"

We found no dwelling-houses anywhere in the midst of the city, until we came to the suburbs. Here they stood in great magnificence and splendor. But one pleasing fact was that every home had its large door-yard, full of trees and flowers and pleasant walks; indeed, it was everywhere, outside of the business center of the town, like one vast park dotted with lovely houses.

There was much that charmed, much that surprised me in this great city, of which I may not fully speak, but which I never can forget. We found in one place a very large park, with walks and drives and fountains and miniature lakes and shaded seats, but no dwellings or buildings of any kind, except an immense circular open temple capable of seating many hundred; and where, my brother told me, a seraph choir assembled at a certain hour daily and rendered the oratorios written by the great musical composers of earth and heaven. It had just departed, and the crowd who had enjoyed its divine music yet lingered as though loath to leave a spot so hallowed.

"We will remember the hour," my brother said, "and come again when we can hear them."

Chapter Fourteen

Not all the archangels can tell
    The joys of that holiest place,
Where the Father is pleased to reveal
    The light of His heavenly face.

- Charles Wesley.

"And the temple was filled with smoke from the glory of God, and from his power." **- Rev. 15: 8.**

Still passing through the park, we came out upon the open country, and walked some distance through flowery meadows and undulating plains. At length we entered a vast forest whose great trees towered above us like swaying giants. The day was well-nigh spent—the day so full of joy and glad surprises and happy hours! Full as it had been I felt there was still something left for me, deep hidden in the twilight-valley of the day; something that held my soul in awe, as the last moments preceding the Holy Sacrament.

My brother walked by me, absorbed in silent thought, but with a touch beyond even his usual gentleness. I did not ask where we were going at that unusual hour, so far from home, for fear and doubt and questionings no longer vexed the quiet of my soul. Although the forest was dense, the golden glow of the twilight rested beneath the trees, and sifted down through the quivering branches overhead, as though falling through the windows of some grand cathedral.

At length we emerged from the forest upon a vast plain that stretched out into illimitable space before us, and far away we faintly heard the thunder of the breaking waves of that immortal sea of which I had heard so much but had not yet seen. But for their faint and distant reverberation the silence about us was intense. We stood a moment upon the verge of the forest, then as we advanced a few steps into the plain I became aware that immediately to our right the ground rose into quite an elevation; and, as I turned, a sight broke upon my bewildered eyes that the eternal years of earth and heaven can never efface. Upon the summit of this gentle slope a Temple stood, whose vast dome, massive pillars and solid walls were of unsullied pearl, and through whose great mullioned windows shone a white radiance that swallowed up the golden glow of the twilight and made it its own. I did not cry aloud nor hide my face, as at former revelations; but I sank slowly to my knees, and, crossing my hands upon my breast, with uplifted face, stilled heart and silent lips, laid my whole being in worship at His feet "who sitteth upon the throne." How long I knelt thus I know not. Even immortal life seemed lost before that greatest of celestial mysteries. At length my brother, who had been silently kneeling beside me, arose, and, lifting me to my feet, whispered gently, "Come."

I felt rather than saw that his face was colorless with the depth of his emotion, and I yielded to his guidance in silence. A long flight of low, broad steps, in gradations, rose from almost where we stood to the very door of the Temple. They, too, were of solid pearl, bordered on either side by channels paved with golden stones through which coursed crystal waters that met and mingled in one stream far out upon the plain. Ascending these steps, we entered the Temple, and for a moment stood in silence. I do not know how it was, but in that brief instant—it may have been longer than I knew—every detail of that wonderful interior was fastened upon my memory as a scene is photographed upon the artist's plate. Heretofore it had taken repeated visits to a room to enable me to describe it correctly in detail, but this, in a lightning's flash, was stamped upon the tablet of my memory indelibly for all time—nay, for eternity.

The immense dome, at that moment filled with a luminous cloud, was upheld by three rows of massive pillars of gold. The walls and floors were of pearl, as also the great platform that filled at least one-third of the Temple upon the eastern side. There were no seats of any kind. The great golden pillars stood like rows of sentinels upon the shining floor. A railing of gold ran entirely around the platform upon the three sides, so that it was inaccessible from the body of the Temple. Beneath this railing, upon the temple-floor, a kneeling-step passed around the platform, also of pearl. In the center of the platform an immense altar of gold arose, supported by seraphs of gold with outspread wings, one at each corner; and underneath it, in a great pearl basin, a fountain of sparkling water played, and I knew intuitively it was the source of the magical river that flowed through the gardens of heaven and bore from us the last stains of death and sin.

Nothing living, beside ourselves, was within the Temple except two persons who knelt with bowed heads beside the altar-rail upon the farther side; but by the altar stood four angels, one upon either side, dressed in flowing garments of white, with long, slim trumpets of gold uplifted in their hands, as though waiting in expectancy the signal for their trumpet call. Long draperies of silvery gossamer hung in heavy folds back of the altar platform. Suddenly, in the moment that we looked, we saw the draperies tremble and glow until

54

a radiance far beyond the splendor of the sun at mid-day shone through them, and the whole Temple was "filled with the glory of the Lord." We saw, in the midst of the luminous cloud that filled the dome, the forms of angelic harpers, and as we dropped with bowed heads beside the altar-rail and hid our faces from the "brightness of His coming," we heard the trumpet-call of the four angels about the altar, and the voices of the celestial harpers as they sang:

"Holy, Holy, Holy, Lord God Almighty!
All thy works shall praise thy name, in earth, and sky, and sea.
Holy, Holy, Holy, merciful and mighty,
God in three persons—blessed Trinity. Amen!"

The voices softly died away; the last notes of the golden trumpets had sounded; "and there was silence in heaven." We knew that the visible glory of the Lord was, for the present, withdrawn from the Temple which is his throne; still we knelt with bowed heads in silent worship before him. When at last we arose I did not lift my eyes while within the Temple; I desired it to remain upon my memory as it appeared when filled with his glory.

We walked some time in silence, I leaning upon my brother's arm, for I yet trembled with emotion. I was surprised that we did not return into the forest, but went still farther out upon the plain. But when I saw that we approached the confluence of the two streams which issued from the fountain beneath the altar, I began to understand that we would return by way of the river, instead of by forest and lake.

We reached the stream, at length, and, stepping into a boat that lay by the shore, we were soon floating with the current toward home. We passed through much beautiful scenery on our course that I had not seen before, and which I resolved I would visit in the future, when leisure from my daily duties would permit. Lovely villas, surrounded by beautiful grounds stretching directly up from the water's edge, lay on both sides of the river, and formed a panorama upon which the eye never tired of resting. Toward the end of the journey we passed my sister's lovely home, and we could plainly see her and her husband drinking in the scene with enraptured eyes, from the window of her own room.

My brother and I were both silent the greater part of the time during our journey homeward, though each noted with observant eyes the signs of happy domestic life by which we were surrounded on every side. The verandas and steps of the homes we passed were full of their happy inmates; glad voices could be constantly heard, and merry shouts of laughter came from the throngs of little children playing everywhere upon the flowery lawns. Once I broke our silence by saying to my brother:

"I have been more than once delightfully surprised to hear the familiar songs of earth reproduced in heaven, but never more so than I was to-day. That hymn has long been a favorite of mine."

55

"These happy surprises do not come by chance," he answered. "One of the delights of this rare life is that no occasion is ever overlooked for reproducing here the pure enjoyments of our mortal life. It is the Father's pleasure to make us realize that this existence is but a continuance of the former life, only without its imperfections and its cares."

"Frank, I believe you are the only one of our friends here who has never questioned me about the dear ones left behind; why is it?"

He smiled a peculiarly happy smile as he answered: "Perhaps it is because I already know more than you could tell me."

"I wondered if it was not so," I said, for I remembered well how my dear father had said, in speaking of my brother upon the first day of my coming, "He stands very near to the Master," and I knew how often he was sent upon missions to the world below.

I lay down upon my couch, on our return, with a heart overflowing with joy and gratitude and love, beyond the power of expression; and it seemed to me the tenderness in the Divine eyes that looked down upon me from the wall was deeper, purer, holier than it had ever been before.

"I will reach the standard of perfection you have set for me, my Savior," I faltered, with clasped hands uplifted to him, "if it takes all my life in heaven and all the help from all the angels of light to accomplish it;" and with these words upon my lips, and his tender eyes resting upon me, I sank into the blissful repose of heaven.

Chapter Fifteen

I shall know the loved who have gone before,
   And joyfully sweet will the meeting be,
When over the river, the peaceful river,
   The Angel of Death shall carry me.

- Nancy A. W. Priest

So much occurred, and so rapidly, from the very hour of my entrance within the beautiful gates, that it is impossible for me to transcribe it all. I have been able only to cull here and there incidents that happened day by day; and in so doing many things I would gladly have related have unconsciously been omitted. Of the many dear friends I met, only a very few have been mentioned, for the reason that, of necessity, such meetings are so similar in many respects that the constant repetition, in detail, would become wearisome. I have aimed principally to give such incidents as would show the beautiful domestic life in that happy world; to make apparent the reverence and love all hearts feel toward the blessed Trinity for every good and perfect gift, and to show forth the marvelous power of the Christ-love even in the life beyond the grave.

This world, strange and new to me, held multitudes of those I had loved in the years gone by, and there was scarcely an hour that did not renew for me the ties that once were severed in the mortal life. I remember that as I was walking one day in the neighborhood of Mrs. Wickham's home, shortly after my first memorable visit there, I was attracted by an unpretentious but very beautiful house, almost hidden by luxuriant climbing rose vines, whose flowers of creamy whiteness were beyond compare with any roses I had yet seen in earth or heaven. Meeting Mrs. Wickham, I pointed to the house and asked: "Who lives there?"

"Suppose you go over and see," she said.

"Is it any one I know?" I asked.

"I fancy so. See, someone is even now at the door as though expecting you."

I crossed over the snowy walk and flowery turf—for the house stood in an angle formed by two paths crossing, almost opposite Mrs. Wickham's—and before I could ascend the steps I found myself in the embrace of two loving arms.

"Bertha Sprague! I was sure it was you when I saw you go to Mrs. Wickham's a day or two ago. Did not she tell you I was here?"

"She had no opportunity until to-day," I said. "But dear Aunt Ann, I should have found you soon; I am sure you know that."

"Yes, I am sure you would."

Then I recounted to her something of my visit to Mrs. Wickham's that eventful day. She listened with her dear face full of sympathy, then said:

"There, dear, you need not tell me. Do I not know? When the Master comes to gladden my eyes, I have no thought or care for anything beyond, for days and days! Oh, the joy, the peace of knowing I am safe in this blessed haven! How far beyond all our earthly dreams is this divine life!"

She sat for a moment lost in thought, then said wistfully: "Now, tell me of my children—are they coming?"

I gladdened her heart with all the cheering news I could bring of her loved ones; and so we talked the hours away, recalling many sweet memories of the earth-life, of friends and home and family ties, and looking forward to the future coming to us of those whom even the joys of heaven could not banish from our hearts.

Then also another evening, as the soft twilight fell, and many of our dear home circle were gathered with us in the great "flower-room," we heard a step upon the veranda, and as my brother went to the open door a gentle voice said:

"Is Mrs. Sprague really here?"

"She is really here. Come and see for yourself." And sweet Mary Green entered the room.

"I am so glad to welcome you home!" she said, coming to me with extended hands, and looking into mine with her tender, earnest eyes.

"My precious girl!" I cried, taking her to my heart in a warm embrace. "I have been asking about you, and longing to see you."

"I could scarcely wait to reach here when I heard that you had come. Now, tell me everything—everything!" she said as I drew her to a seat close beside me.

But questions asked and the answers given are too sacred for rehearsal here. Every individual member of her dear home-circle was discussed, and many were the incidents she recounted to me that had occurred in her presence when her mother and I were together and talking of the dear child we considered far removed from our presence.

"I was often so close that I could have touched you with my hand, had the needed power been given," she said.

After a long, close converse had been held between us, I took her to the library, whither the rest had gone to examine a new book just that day received. I introduced her to them all as the daughter of dear friends still on earth, confident of the welcome she would receive. My youngest sister and she at once became interested in each other, finding congeniality in many of their daily pursuits, and I was glad to believe they would henceforth see much of each other in many different ways.

There was no measurement of time as we measure it here, although many still spoke in the old-time language of "months" and "days" and "years." I have no way of describing it as it seemed to me then. There were periods, and allotted times; there were hours for happy duties, hours for joyful pleasures, and hours for holy praise. I only know it was all harmony, all joy, all peace, at all times and in all conditions.

Chapter Sixteen

There is an endearing tenderness in the love of a mother to a son, that transcends all other affections of the heart. It is neither to be chilled by selfishness, nor daunted by danger, nor weakened by worthlessness, nor stifled by ingratitude. She will sacrifice every comfort to his convenience; she will surrender every pleasure to his enjoyment; she will glory in his fame, and exult in his prosperity; and if adversity overtake him, he will be the dearer to her by misfortune; and if disgrace settle upon his name, she will still love and cherish him; and if all the world beside cast him off, she will be all the world to him. - Washington Irving.

The current of my life flowed on in the heavenly ways, until the months began to lengthen into years and my daily studies ascended higher in the scale of celestial mysteries. I never wearied of study, though much was taught and gained through the medium of observation in the journeys that I was permitted to take with my brother into different parts of the heavenly kingdom. I never lacked time for social pleasures and enjoyments, for there is no clashing of duties with inclination, no unfulfilled desires, no vain strivings for the unattainable in that life, as in the life of earth. Many precious hours of intercourse were spent in my dear father's home, and sometimes on rare occasions I was permitted to accompany him to his field of labor and assist him in instructing those lately come into the new life with little or no preparation for its duties and responsibilities. On one occasion he said to me:

"I have the most difficult problem to deal with I have ever yet met in this work. It is how to enlighten and help a man who suddenly plunged from an apparently honorable life into the very depths of crime. I have never been able to get him to accompany me to the river, where these earthly cobwebs would be swept from his poor brain; his excuse being always that God's mercy is so great in allowing him inside heaven's gates at all, that he is content to remain always in its lowest scale of enjoyment and life. No argument or teaching thus far can make him alter his decision. He was led astray by infatuation for a strange woman, and killed his aged mother in order to secure her jewels for this wretched creature. He was executed for the crime, of which in the end he sincerely repented, but he left life with all the horror of the deed clinging to his soul."

"Has he seen his mother since coming here? Does she know of his arrival?"

"No; she is entirely alone in this world, and it was not thought wise to tell her of his coming till his soul was in a better condition to receive her. He was an only child, and does not lack the elements of refinement, but he was completely under the control of this vile though fascinating woman. It is said she drugged his wine and incited him to do the dreadful deed while under its influence, because of her hatred for his mother, whose influence was against her. When he came from under the influence of the wine, he was horrified at what he had done, and his infatuation for the woman turned to loathing— but, alas, too late! He would not see her during his entire incarceration."

"How long was he in prison?"

"Almost a year."

"Has he seen the Christ?"

"No; he begs not to see him. He is very repentant, and grateful to be saved from the wrath he feels was his just punishment, but though he is conscious that his sin is forgiven, he does not yet feel that he can ever stand in the presence of the Holy One. And here, as upon earth, each must be willing to receive him. His presence is never given undesired. I have not yet appealed for higher help; my ambition is to lead these weak souls upward through the strength entrusted to me. Can you suggest anything that would probably reach him?"

"His mother. May I bring her?"

He thought a moment reflectively, then said: "A woman's intuition. Yes, bring her."

"O sweet and blessed country,
"O sweet and blessed country,
"O sweet and blessed country,
    The home of God's elect!
O sweet and blessed country

That eager hearts expect!
There stand those halls of Zion
　All jubilant with song,
And bright with many an angel,
　And all the martyr throng."

I soon was on my way. I found the poor woman, laid the facts gently before her, and waited her decision. There was no hesitancy upon her part; in an instant she said, "My poor boy! Certainly I will go with you at once."

We found my father waiting for us, and went immediately to the great "Home" where these "students"—would we call them?—stayed. It was a beautiful great building in the midst of a park, with shaded walks and fountains and flowers everywhere. To one just freed from earth it seemed a paradise indeed; but to those of us who had tasted heaven's rarer joys, something was wanting. We missed the lovely individual homes, the little children playing on the lawns, the music of the angel choir; it was tame indeed beside the pleasures we had tasted.

We found the young man seated beneath one of the flower-laden trees, intently perusing a book that my father had left with him. There was a peaceful look on his pale face, but it was rather the look of patient resignation than of ardent joy. His mother approached him alone; my father and I remaining in the background. After a little time he glanced up and saw his mother standing near him. A startled look came into his face, and he rose to his feet. She extended her arms toward him, and cried out pathetically, "John, my dear boy, come home to me—I need you!" That was all.

With a low cry he knelt at her feet and clasped her knees, sobbing: "Mother! mother!"

She stooped and put her tender arms about him; she drew his head gently to her breast and showered kisses on his bowed head. Oh, the warm mother-love, the same in earth and heaven! Only the Christ-love can exceed it. Here was this outraged mother, sent into eternity by the hands of him who should have shielded and sustained her, bending above her repentant son with the mother-love with which her heart was overflowing shining upon him from her gentle eyes. I saw my father turn his head to conceal his emotion, and I knew that my own eyes were wet. My father had explained to the mother that the first thing to be accomplished was to get her son to the river, so we now heard her say caressingly:

"Come, John, my boy, take the first step upward, for your mother's sake, that in time I may have the joy of seeing you in our own home. Come, John, with mother."

She gently drew him, and to our great joy we saw him rise and go with her, and their steps led them to the river. They walked hand in hand, and as far as we could see them she seemed to be soothing and comforting him.

"Thank God!" said my father fervently. "There will be no further trouble now. When they return he will see with clearer vision." And so it proved.

After this, by divine permission, I became much of the time a co-laborer with my father, and thus enjoyed his society and his instructions much oftener than otherwise I could have done.

Chapter Seventeen

"Some day," we say, and turn our eyes
Toward the fair hills of Paradise;
Some day, some time, a sweet new rest
Shall blossom, flower-like, in each breast.
Some day, some time, our eyes shall see
The faces kept in memory;
Some day their hand shall clasp our hand,
Just over in the Morning-land—
O Morning-land! O Morning-land!

- Edward H. Phelps.

One evening, some three years—counted by the calendar of earth—after I had entered upon the joys and duties of the heavenly life, I sat resting upon the upper veranda of our home, after a somewhat arduous journey to a distant city of the heavenly realm. From this part of the veranda we caught rare glimpses of the river through the overhanging branches of the trees; and just below us, at a little distance, we could see the happy children at their play upon the lawn. Here my brother sought me out, and throwing himself upon a soft veranda lounge near, lay for a time motionless and silent. He looked as wearied as one can ever look in that life, but I felt no anxiety about him, for I knew the rest was sure. He had been absent on some earth-mission much of the time for many days, and I knew from experience that some of the fatigue and care of earth will cling to us on such occasions, till we are restored by heaven's balmy air and life-giving waters. He had not told me, as he sometimes did, where his mission had led him, and I had not asked him, feeling sure that all it was best I should know would be imparted. My own duties had of late been unusually responsible, leading me daily to a distant part of the heavenly kingdom, hence I myself had not visited the beloved of earth for a much longer period than usually elapsed between my visits. When last seen, all of the dear ones had seemed in such vigorous health and were so surrounded by earthly blessings that I had ceased to feel they needed my ministrations as in the early days of their sorrow, hence I had thrown all of my energies into the work assigned me by the Master.

At length, after a time of rest, my brother arose to a sitting posture, and regarding me for a moment in silence, said gently: "I have news for you, little sister."

A thrill like an electric shock passed through me, and in an instant I cried out joyously: "He is coming!"

He nodded his head, with a sympathetic smile, but did not at once reply.

"When will it be? Am I to go to him?" I asked.

He hesitated an instant before saying: "Of course you are permitted to go, if your heart will not be denied."

"Oh, I must go to him! I must be the first to greet him! Perhaps it may be granted him to see me even while he is yet in the flesh."

He shook his head sadly at this, and said, "No, dear; he will not know you."

"Why? Frank, tell me all—and why you think, as I plainly see you do, that it is not best I should go."

"He was stricken suddenly in the midst of his work, while apparently in perfect health, and has not regained consciousness since; nor will he ever on earth. Hence your presence could be no solace to him."

"When was this?"

"Three days ago; I have been with him almost constantly by day and night ever since."

"Oh, why did you not sooner tell me?"

"It was thought wise to spare you the unnecessary pain of seeing him suffer when you could not minister to him, and I have come to tell you now that you may go if you still so desire."

"He will know me as soon as the struggle is past?"

"Yes, but he will be bewildered and weak; he will need stronger help and guidance than you alone can give, and you will miss the rapture of the meeting as it would be a little later on."

"What would you have me do? You know I will yield to your wiser judgment even against the pleadings of my heart. But I can wait!"

"I will not say, 'do not go.' You shall accompany me if you wish. I only think that after the first bewilderment of the change has passed, after he has bathed in the waters of the River of Life, he will be better prepared for the delightful reunion which awaits him. You remember what the waters did for you, and how bewildered and oppressed in spirit you were till you went with me that morning, into the river. It is the same with all of us, only where there has been serious trouble with the brain at last, it is even more needed than on ordinary occasions. And that is the case with my brother; he will not be fully himself until the magical waters have swept the clouds from his brain."

"You are always right, my brother, and I will yield to your wise advice, although my heart cries out to hasten at once to his side. When will you return to him?"

"Immediately. There will be little time to wait. With the quickening of the morning light we will be here. My brave-hearted, wise little sister, the delay will be to you neither sorrowful nor long."

He arose, and, bending over me, dropped a kiss lightly on my brow, and in a moment he had passed from my sight.

"How strange," I thought, "that even in this matter, so near to my heart, I am able to yield unmurmuringly! Father, I thank Thee! I thank Thee for the glad reunion so near at hand; but, even more than that, for the sweet submission in all things that has grown into my life; that I can yield to Thy will even when Thou wouldst permit it to be otherwise."

I bowed my head upon my hand and gave myself up to mingled sad and happy thoughts. Was he, this dearly loved one, indeed insensible to his suffering? Would the Father mercifully spare him even the pang of the parting? Oh, that the morning were here! How could I wait even that brief while for the sight of the beloved face!

Suddenly a soft touch rested upon my bowed head, and a Voice I had learned to recognize and love beyond all things in earth or heaven said: "Have I not said truly, 'Though he were dead, yet shall he live again'? What are now the years of separation, since the meeting again is at hand? Come, and let us reason a little together," the Master said, smiling down into my uplifted face. He took my extended hand into his own, and sitting down beside me, continued:

"Let us consider what these years have done for you. Do you not feel that you are infinitely better prepared to confer happiness than when you parted from him you love?"

I nodded in glad affirmation.

"Do you not realize that you stand upon a higher plane, with more exalted ideas of life and its duties; and that, in the strength of the Father, you two henceforward will walk upward together?"

Again I gladly acquiesced.

"Is the home-life here less attractive than it was in the earth-life?"

"No, no! A thousand times no!" I cried.

"Then there is nothing but joy in the reunion at hand?"

"Nothing but joy," I echoed.

Then the Savior led me on to talk of the one so soon to come, and I opened my glad heart to him and told him of the noble life, the unselfish toil, the high aspirations, the unfaltering trust of him I loved. I spoke of his fortitude in misfortune, his courage in the face of sore trial and disappointment, his forgiveness of even malicious injury; and concluded by saying, "He lived the Christianity many others professed. He always distanced me in that."

The face of the Master glowed in sympathy as I talked, and when I ceased he said: "I perceive that you have discovered the secret which makes marriage eternal as the years of heaven."

"Oh," I said, "to me marriage must be eternal! How could it be otherwise when two grow together and become as one? Death cannot separate them without destroying; they are no longer two perfect beings, but one in soul and spirit forever."

"Aye," he answered; "but having the marriage rite pronounced does not produce this change. It is the divinity of soul wedded to soul alone that can do it."

So he led me on until my soul flew upward as a lark in the early morning. He unfolded to me mysteries of the soul-life that filled my heart with rapture, but which I may not here reveal. At length, to my infinite surprise, I saw the rosy glow deepening across the sky, and knew that morning—love's morning—had dawned for me in heaven. The Master arose, and pointing to the radiance, said: "By the time thou art ready to receive them they will be here;" and with a smile, and a touch that made a benediction, he departed.

As I arose and stood with face uplifted to the coming day, I caught in the near distance the triumphant notes of the angels' choral song; and this morning, as though in sympathy with my thought, they sang:

"He is risen! Hear it, ye heavens, and ye sons of earth! He is risen, and has become the first fruits of them that slept!"

I lifted up my voice with joy, and joined their thrilling song; and as they swept onward and the cadence died away, I slowly descended the stairway, crossed the lawn whose flowers never crushed or withered beneath our feet, and sank for a moment beneath the pure waters of the river. I felt no haste, no unwonted excitement or unrest, though I knew that he was coming for whom my soul had waited all these years. The Master's presence had filled me with calm and peace that nothing had power to disturb; had prepared and fitted me for the great happiness lying just before me.

Uplifted with a new, strange delight, I recrossed the lawn, stopping upon the veranda before entering the house, to gather a knot of cream-white roses and fasten them to my breast. Then going to the library, I refilled the golden bowl with the spicy-breathed scarlet carnations, laying one aside to fasten upon my husband's shoulder. I wanted to myself gather the flowers that would greet him on his coming. I twisted up my hair in the manner that he had most admired, and fastened a creamy bud within the folds, that I might seem to him as I had of old.

Soon thereafter I heard voices and steps. Listen! Yes, it is the same dear step for which I had so often listened in the old home-life, the step that had always brought gladness to my heart, and sunshine in our home! His step in heaven! I flew to the open doorway, and in an instant was held close in the strong arms and to the loving, throbbing heart of my dear husband. Was there anything more for me that heaven could give!

My brother, with thoughtful care, passed onward to the upper rooms of the house, and for awhile we were alone together, we whose lives had run, so happily mingled, through the long years of our mortal life. I drew him within the house, and in the vestibule again he took me in his arms and drew me to his heart.

"This is heaven indeed!" he said.

We passed into the "flower-room," and on its threshold he stood a moment, entranced with its beauty; but when I would have related to him its history, as my brother had given it to me, he said: "Not to-day, my dear; I have only eyes and ears for you to-day; all else in heaven must wait."

So we sat and talked together as in the olden days, and the happy hours came and went, and the day melted into the twilight glow, before we realized it was half spent. Our brother Frank had come to us about the noontide, and together we had gone over the lovely house, had stood upon the broad verandas and eaten of the heavenly fruit. Then we all sat together where I had spent the hours waiting in the presence of the blessed Master. I told them much that he then had said to me, and how he turned into triumphant rejoicing the hours which I had anticipated would pass in lonely waiting. The eyes of my dear husband were tear-filled, and he pressed my hand, which he still kept in his, in tender sympathy.

"Oh, darling, it is a blessed, blessed life!" I said.

"I already realize the blessedness," he replied, "for has it not given me back my brother and my wife—my precious wife!"

Early the following morning I said to my husband and our brother: "We must go to father and mother Sprague's to-day. They have the first claim, after ours, Frank."

"Yes, we will go at once," they both replied.

So together we all started. In the earliest days of my heavenly life I had sought out with much joy the home of my husband's parents, and was by them accorded, as in the earth-life, a warm place in their hearts, and many happy hours had we spent together since. Now we were taking to them a favorite son, and I realized how his coming would bring gladness to their hearts and home. It was a joyful meeting, especially to our mother, and the day was far spent before we arose to return.

"William," said our mother, fondly laying her hand upon his arm, "yours was a happy home on earth—I used to think a perfect home; it will be far happier here," with a loving glance at me.

"I am sure of that, mother. I have my dear wife and Frank constantly with me; and you and my father and Josephine"—a favorite niece—"to come to here; and after awhile," with a little hesitation, "the holier joys and privileges of heaven."

We turned to go, and upon the threshold met an aunt who in the earth-life—blind and helpless—had been a favorite with us all.

"My dear children," she exclaimed, "how good it seems to see you all again!"

"Aunt Cynthia!" my husband said fondly.

"Yes, Aunt Cynthia, but no longer groping helpless in the darkness. 'Whereas I once was blind, now I see,'" she quoted, smiling happily.

And so it was—the Master's touch had rested on the sightless eyes, and, closing to the darkness of earth, they had opened upon the glories of heaven. Marvelous transition! No wonder we left her singing:

Glory to Him who this marvel hath wrought,
Filling my spirit with joy and delight!
Lo, in my blindness I safely have walked
Out of the darkness into the light!

Chapter Eighteen

Down by the sea, the crystal sea,
Where all of the redeemed shall be,
Where you and I, beloved, shall go,
Our crimson robes washed white as snow
In Christ's dear blood—what hymns of praise
Thro' countless ages we shall raise!
There all our loved ones we shall see—
Think what a meeting that will be
Down by the sea!

- From "Songs by the Sea."

Days lengthened into weeks, and weeks into months, and these in turn crept onward into years, and the duties and joys of heaven grew clearer and dearer with each passing hour. Our home-life was perfect, though we looked forward with joy to the future coming of our son and daughter to make its ties complete. We had often spoken of going together to the great celestial sea, but the time had never seemed quite ripe for so doing. We realized it was one of the great mysteries of heaven, although we knew not just what to expect, since there no one ever seeks to forestall sight by description. One evening I said to my brother:

"I have a strange desire to go to the sea, if you think it wise that we should do so."

"I am glad that it is your desire to go, as it is mine to have you. I was about to propose that you and my brother should take together this blessed journey."

"Will you not accompany us?"

"Not at this time. We will all take it again together, but it is best that now you two should go alone. You know the way. Through the forest that leads to the Temple, till almost there; then bear to the right and follow the golden path that takes you direct to the shore."

So, in the quivering light of the glorious morning we started, full of a holy joy that together we might take this special journey. We entered and traversed the great forest, where the golden light fell through the quivering branches overhead, and birds of gorgeous plumage and thrilling song were darting everywhere. We heard, nearer and ever nearer, the regular dashing of the waves against the shore; and now there came to us bursts of triumphant song and the harmony of many instruments of music. At length we emerged from the forest, and stood mute and motionless before the overwhelming glory of the scene before us.

Can I describe it as it appeared to me that day? Never, until my lips can speak, and your heart understand, the language of the royal courts above. From our very feet sloped downward toward the shore a golden strand many hundred feet wide, and extending on either hand far beyond the limits of our vision. This strand caught and radiated the morning light until wherever it was visible it glittered and glimmered like the dust of diamonds and other precious stones, and the waves, as they came and went in ceaseless motion, caught up this sparking sand and carried it on their crests, like the phosphorescence we sometimes see in the wake of a vessel in mid-ocean. And the sea! It spread out before us in a radiance that passes description in any language I have ever known. It was like the white glory that shone through the windows of the Temple, and beneath this shining glory we caught in the roll of the waves the blue tint of the waters of that sea which has no limit to its depths or bounds. Upon its shining bosom we saw in every direction boats, representing all nations, but in beauty of construction far surpassing anything earth has ever known. They were like great open pleasure-barges, and were filled with people looking with eager faces toward the shore, many in their eagerness standing erect and gazing with wistful, expectant eyes into the faces of those upon the shore.

Ah, the people upon the shore! "Numberless as the sands of the sea," they stood, far as the eye could reach, far as stretched the shore of that illimitable sea, a great mass of beautiful souls clad in the spotless garments of the redeemed. Many among them had golden harps and various instruments of music, and whenever a boat touched the shore and its inmates were welcomed by the glad voices and tender embraces of their beloved ones in the throng, the harps would be held aloft, all of the golden instruments would sound, and the vast multitude would break forth into the triumphant song of victory over death and the grave.

"Do these people stand here always, I wonder?" I said softly.

"Not the same people," said a radiant being near us, who had heard my question. "But there is always a throng of people here—those who are expecting friends from the other life, and those who assemble to share their joy. Some of the heavenly choristers also are always here, but not always the same ones. You will notice that most of those who arrive are led quietly away by their friends, and many others are constantly joining the multitude."

He passed onward toward the shore, and left us rapt in awe and wonder.

We soon became deeply interested in watching the reunions, and found ourselves joining with rapture in the glad songs of rejoicing. Now and then a face we remembered to have seen on earth would be among the eager faces in the boats, but none that had been especially dear to us; still it made us notice more closely and sympathize more heartily with those who welcomed beloved friends. Now we would see a wife caught in the close embrace of a waiting husband; now a little child with a glad cry would spring into the outstretched arms of the happy mother; friend would clasp friend in glad reunion, and here an aged mother would be folded to the heart of a beloved child.

As one boat of more than usual strength and beauty came riding gracefully over the waves, we observed the tall figure of a man standing near her prow with his arms about a graceful woman who stood by his side. Each shaded with uplifted hand from their dazzled eyes the unwonted splendor and scanned, wistfully and searchingly, the faces of the crowd as the boat neared the shore. Suddenly with a great thrill of joy surging through my being, I cried out:

"It is our precious son, and his dear wife! And they have come together!"

In an instant we were swiftly moving through the throng that parted in ready sympathy to let us pass. And, as the boat touched the shore, with a swift movement they were both beside us—the dear daughter already close clasped to the hearts of her own happy parents who were waiting near the water's edge, while at the same instant we felt the arms of our beloved son enfolding us; and soon thereafter we were all in each other's embrace. Oh, what a rapturous moment was that! Our home life in heaven complete, no partings forever! As we stood with encircling arms, scarcely realizing the unexpected bliss, the heavenly choir broke into song; and with uplifted faces radiant with joy, eyes filled with happy tears and voices trembling with emotion, we all joined in the glad anthem:

Glory be unto the Father, and unto the Son!
Glory be unto the ever-blessed Three in One!
No more sorrow, no more parting, no more grief or pain;
Christ has broken death's strong fetters, we are free again!
Heart to heart and hand to hand,
Meet we on the golden strand.
Glory, glory to the Father! Glory to the Son!
Glory be unto the ever-blessed Three in One!
Alleluia! Amen!

The song rose and swelled triumphantly as the vast multitude caught it up, and the surge of the waves made a deep undertone to the melody that increased its solemnity, as with bowed heads and full hearts we passed onward hand in hand; and the light that fell about us was purer, holier, more divine, than it had ever been before.

Chapter Nineteen

Can such things be,
And overcome us like a summer's cloud,
Without our special wonder?

- Shakespeare.

A time came when one day as I stood in my lovely room that had really become to me a shrine, and looked up into the pictured face of the Christ above me, I fancied that the tender eyes looking down into mine no longer told of a deathless love alone, but carried in their depths a pity, a loving compassion which I had never noticed there before. Then as I turned toward my couch I even fancied that his hands reached out from the canvas and rested in benediction on my head. I stood a moment in blessed peace before him, then as the hands seemed to be withdrawn, I turned and lay down for an instant's rest. But strange thoughts and fancies crept into my brain, such as I had not known in years. I felt confused and bewildered, and started up restlessly from my pillow, only to fall back again in doubt, and something akin to dread. What could it mean? Could the old unrest of earth find place in this divine retreat? Then I heard unfamiliar voices. Someone said:

"Her color is better than it has been for several days, I think."

"Yes, there is no doubt but she is better to-day. There is really hope for her now, I am sure. But she came very near passing through the Gates."

"Very near passing through the Gates"! As though I had not passed through, and in returning left them so ajar that gleams of the heavenly radiance from beyond them will fall about my life forever!

I have been in my Father's house.

"We shall know each other there!"

Supplemental Chapter

In the many letters received since the publication of "Intra Muros," repeated inquiries have been made of me on different points contained in the book, requiring much correspondence, and it has been suggested that possibly the addition of a few pages, as a supplement to the book, might explain some matters, or, possibly, make more clear some points that have not been fully comprehended by the reader.

Let me in the beginning reassert what I have heretofore stated: that I have never claimed that this strange experience is either a revelation or an inspiration. It came to me during a period of great physical suffering and prostration, and I have always considered it as sent in compensation for that suffering. Be this as it may, it has been a great comfort and help to me, and, through the letters received from others, I am led to believe it has been the same to many who have read it, for which cause I am extremely gratified. I wish that I might give the entire experience just as it came to me, but I find that earth-language is wholly inadequate for me to do so. There were so many mysteries, so many teachings far beyond anything that in this life we have known, that I find myself bewildered and lost when I attempt to convey to others the marvelous things that at that time seemed indeed to me to be a most wonderful revelation.

The question has repeatedly been asked me, "Was this a real experience, or merely a fanciful sketch?" What I have written above will as nearly answer that question as it is possible for me to do. The preface and early pages as given in the little volume are as nearly accurate as I can make them; and anything that I might add on that point would simply be superfluous. To me, at the time, it was as real as any experience in this life could possibly be.

Questions have been asked respecting the comparative distances in heaven and our powers of passing from one point to another; and the question has even been asked if in the other life we developed wings that aided us in passage, as the wings of a bird. These matter-of-fact questions are sometimes quite difficult to answer, for my belief is, that if I were really in the other life, as during this experience I seemed to be, my thoughts would be so far above, so lifted beyond such temporal matters, that I would be unable to answer such inquiries satisfactorily on my return to this life. Looking back upon it now, and trying to gather facts from the impressions that I then received, I should say that none who have ever passed through mortal life would in any way be changed from their present personal appearance, except to be etherealized and glorified. When I seemed to stand in that wonderful Temple filled with the Glory of God the Father, four angels with uplifted trumpets stood beside the golden altar on the great platform of pearl, and from their shoulders shadowy pinions enfolded them and touched the floor upon which they stood. And when, in a moment of bewildering emotion, I lifted my eyes to the erstwhile cloud-filled dome, I saw about the hitherto invisible choir, the shadowy pinions of which we so often read, half concealing the harps and instruments of gold. Also, when at the close of that wonderful day when I had first met the Savior, we heard the angel voices as we stood together in the great flower-room, and, looking upward, saw the child faces in the golden twilight above us, they, too, had delicate shadowy wings, half concealing the baby forms. Except for this, I have no recollection of having seen any of those glorious wings of which we so often read.

To me it seems that to the angels of God who have always lived in heaven, these are given; but to those who have suffered and toiled and borne the cross below, is given only the glorified form, such as our Savior himself bore. We appear to our friends when we meet them over there just as they saw us here, only purified and perfect. Still, we had powers of locomotion given us that carried us from point to point swiftly and securely, as though borne by a boat upon the waters.

I do not know how I can better illustrate this point than by giving a little incident not mentioned in the book. I remember, as I sat one morning upon the upper terrace in the house of my sister whom I had welcomed there soon after my arrival, and who, though really then a denizen of earth, has since passed over and taken possession of that beautiful home prepared for her, that my sister said to me:

"I often look across the river to those lovely hills in the distance, and wonder if it is all as beautiful there as here. I mean some day to go and see."

"Why not go to-day?" was my answer.

70

"Could you go with me this morning?" was her inquiry, as she turned her radiant face again toward the river and the lovely fields beyond.

"With pleasure," I replied. "I have often wished to go myself. There is something very inviting in the beautiful landscape beyond the river. Where is my brother Oliver?" I asked; "will he not accompany us?"

"No," she said, looking smilingly toward me, "he has gone upon an important mission for the Master to-day; but you and I, dear, can go, and be at home again before his return."

"Then let us do so," I replied, rising and giving her my hand.

She at once arose, and, instead of turning toward the stairway in the center of the building, we turned and walked deliberately to the low coping that surrounded the upper veranda. Without a moment's hesitation we stepped over this into the sweet air that lay about us. There was no more fear of falling than if our feet had been upon the solid earth. We had the power of passing through the air at will, and through the water, just as we had the power of walking upon the crystal paths and greensward about us.

We ascended slightly until we were just above the tree-tops, and then—what shall I say?—we did not fly, we made no effort either with our hands or our feet; I can only think of the word "drifting" that will at all describe this wonderful experience. We went as a leaf or a feather floats through the air on a balmy day, and the sensation was most delightful. We saw beneath us through the green branches of the trees the little children playing, and the people walking—some for pleasure, some for duty. As we neared the river we looked down on the pleasure-boats upon the water and upon the people sitting or lying or walking on the pebbly bottom; and we saw them with the same distinctness as though we were looking at them simply through the atmosphere.

Conversing as we drifted onward, we soon were over the tops of the hills to which we had looked so longingly from the veranda of my sister's house, and, for some time, we had no words to exchange; our hearts were filled with sensations such as only the scenes of heaven can give. Then my sister said very softly, quoting from one of the old earth-hymns:
"Sweet fields beyond the swelling flood.
Stand dressed in living green."

And, in the same spirit, I answered, "It is indeed a rapturous scene—
"'That rises to our sight,
Sweet fields arrayed in living green, and rivers of delight.'"

As we passed onward, in looking down we began to see many suburban villages, similar to that in which our own happy homes were situated. Among many of them there was an unfamiliar air, and the architecture of the buildings in many respects seemed quite different from our own. I suggested to my sister that we drop downward a little. On doing so, we soon realized what caused this apparent difference in the architecture and surroundings. Where our homes were situated we were surrounded by people we had known and loved on earth, and of our own nationality. Many of these villages over which we were now passing we found were formed from what, to us, would be termed of foreign nations, and each village retained some of the peculiarities of its earth-life, and these, to us, were naturally unfamiliar. We recognized again the wisdom and goodness of the Father in thus allowing friends of the same nationality to be located near each other in heaven, as on earth.

As we still drifted onward, in passing over an exquisitely beautiful valley, between low hills of the most enchanting verdure, we saw a group of people seated upon the ground in a semicircle. They seemed to be hundreds in number, and in their midst a man was standing who, apparently, was talking to them. Something familiar, and yet unfamiliar, in the scene attracted us, and I said, "Let us go nearer, and hear, if possible, what he is saying, and see who these people are."

Upon doing this we found the people to resemble in a great measure our own Indian tribes; their dress, in a manner, corresponding to that worn upon earth, though so etherealized as to be surpassingly beautiful. But the dusky faces and the long black hair still remained. The faces, with intense interest depicted on each, were turned toward the man who, we could see, was talking to them, and, looking upon him, we saw at once that he belonged to the Anglo-Saxon race. In a whisper of surprise I said to my sister:

"Why, he is a missionary!"

As so often seemed to me to happen in that experience, when a surprise or a difficulty presented itself, there was always some one near to answer and enlighten us. And so we found on this occasion that our instructor was beside us ready to answer any surprise or question that might be asked. He said at once:

"Yes, you are right. This is a missionary who gave his life to what on earth were called the heathen. He spent many years in working for them and enlightening those who sat in darkness, with the result, as you see before you, of bringing hundreds into the kingdom of the Master. But, as you will naturally suppose, they have much to learn, and here he still gathers them about him, and day by day leads them higher and higher into the blessed life."

"Are there many such," I asked, "doing this work in this beautiful realm?"

"Many hundreds," he said. "To these poor minds, unenlightened as they were when they first came, heaven is as beautiful and happy a place as it is to any who have ascended higher, simply because we can enjoy only in the capacity to which our souls can reach. There are none of us who have not much yet to learn of this wonderful country."

In several instances, as we drifted across above the villages, we heard songs of praise arising from the temples, and from people collected in different ways. In many cases, to our surprise, the hymns and the words were those with which we had been familiar on earth, and, although sung in a strange tongue, we understood them all. That was another of the wonderful surprises of heaven. There was no language there that we could not understand.

On, and on, and on, through wonderful scenes of beauty we passed, returning finally to our own homes by a different way from that by which we had gone forth, seeming to have made almost a circle in our pleasant journeyings. When I left my sister in her own home she whispered to me as she bade me good-by for the present:

"It has been a day of such wonderful rest and pleasure that we must soon repeat it together." And I answered:

"Yes, dear, we will."

In several instances the subject of dual marriages has been introduced. More than once it has been suggested, "If a man marrying in early life, and, being devotedly attached to the woman he has married, should unfortunately lose her, and after many years of solitary waiting find another congenial soul to whom his whole heart goes out and marriage is the result, and they have many years of wedded happiness together before she, too, is called, to whom will he belong in the other life?"

In the many phases of the divine life that seemed to come to me in my vision, such thoughts as the above were never by any means suggested. Speaking from my own natural intuitions, I cannot but think that as soon as the immortal part of us leaves the earthly tenement, it lays down forever, with that tenement, all thoughts that embarrassed or grieved or pained the spirit. In the homes of heaven there was perpetual love and joy and peace and happiness without measure. This one thing I know: In heaven are no conflicting ties; no questions that vex; no conditions that annoy; the whole heart springs up to do the will of the Father, and nothing less than that will suffice.

In answer to the question in many instances proposed to me, as to whether I consider this experience as a revelation, I can only say, as heretofore, that I gave it as it came to me, and every one must draw his own inference concerning it. I can be the guide for no one.

There are some seeming inconsistencies in the book, of which I myself am aware. Looking back upon it after nearly four years have passed, it seems to me to be more a series of instructions such as we give little children here in a kindergarten. It does not purport to be a revelation of what has been or what will be, in the strict sense of the word, but, as I have already suggested, more as we would teach children in a kindergarten. I myself noticed, in transcribing this strange experience, the fact that the first lesson to be taught almost invariably came as an illustration; and, after my wonder and pleasure had taken in all that the picture itself would teach, then followed the revelation, or a general application of its meaning. For instance, that I may make my meaning more clear: When I myself first entered within the gates, I was shown the wonders of the celestial gardens and the magic of the beautiful river; then the meeting with the dear ones from whom I had been so long parted. And so I came to know the rapture of the disembodied spirit on its first entrance "Within the Walls." Afterwards followed the instruction or first lessons concerning this life into which I seemed to have entered, until, as I said, the first illustrations and the instructions formed for me but one perfect lesson. And when, as time passed, I met and welcomed my dear sister, my husband and my son, I knew the other side of the question—the joy that came even to the angels in heaven when they welcomed the beloved ones who came to them from the world below. And so, all through the book, the instruction was invariably preceded by the illustration. Thus I can but think, if any meaning can be attached to this strange vision, that it is simply a lesson in a general way of what we may expect and hope for when we reach the thither shore.

Again, the question is many times repeated, "Does this experience retain its vividness as time passes, or does it grow unreal and dreamlike to you?" I can partially forget some of the happiest experiences of my earth-life, but time seems only to intensify to me the wonders of those days when my feet really stood upon the border-land of the two worlds. It seemed to me that at every step we took in the divine life our souls reached up toward something better, and we had no inclination to look behind to that which had passed, or to try to solve what in our mortal life had been intricate or perplexing questions or mysteries. Like the cup that is filled to overflowing at the fountain with pure and sparkling water, so our souls were filled—more than filled—with draughts from the fountain of all good, until there was no longer room for aught else. "How then," you ask, "could you reach out for more, when you had all that you could receive?" Because moment by moment, hour by hour, our souls grew and expanded and opened to receive fresh draughts of divine instruction which was constantly lifting us nearer to the source of all perfection.

Some of the letters that have come to me have been so pathetic in their inquiries, that they have called forth sympathetic tears, and an intense longing to speak with authority upon the questions raised. That privilege God has not given me. I can only tell how it seemed to me in those blissful hours when earth seemed remote and heaven very near and real. One suffering mother writes, "Do you think I could pray still for my darling girl?" How I longed to take her in sympathetic arms and whisper to her that the dear child of her love, I doubted not, was praising God continually and had no longer need of earthly prayer. She loved and trusted the Savior as she went down into the Valley of Shadows, and his loving arms received and comforted her. To all such I would say—and many are the letters of like import received:

"Look up, dear friends, and see the loved ones, as I saw those so dear to me, happy and blessed beyond all human conception in the house of many mansions prepared for us by our loving Father." Oh, those wonderful mansions upon which my longing heart looks back! Believe in them, look forward to them, beloved friends, for we have the Savior's promise that they at least are there: "In my Father's house are many mansions." His promises never fail; and I am sure of one thing they will not be less beautiful than those I looked upon in my vision.

This thought, to me, answers in a measure the questions asked in regard to dual marriages. My own belief, of this mortal life, is, that no two friends can occupy the same place in our hearts. Each heart is filled with chambers stately and old, and to each beloved guest is assigned a chamber exclusively for himself. That room is always his. If death, or distance, or even disgrace, separates him from us, still the room is his and his only forever. No other person can ever occupy it. Others may have rooms equally choice, but when a guest has once departed from the room he has held in another heart, the door of that room is barred forever; it is held inviolate—sacred to the departed guest. And so, in heaven, each guest has his separate room or home. "In my Father's house are many mansions. I go to prepare a place (room) for you."

I am no advocate of second marriages. The thought of two lives alone as one, is beautiful to me; but I do not, all the same, believe that a man sins against the memory of a wife beloved and lost, when he places by her side (not in her place) a good woman to cheer and brighten his home. She cannot, if she would, take the place left vacant in his home and heart; it is inviolate. I speak, of course, of true marriages, where not only hands are joined, but hearts and souls are knit together as one forever.

"What are the duties of heaven?" So many and varied, I should judge, as to make the question unanswerable. Much in "Intra Muros" shows the trend of daily life.

"Rest?" One of the duties as well as the pleasures of heaven. Rest does not of necessity mean inactivity. How often in this life does laying aside of one duty and taking up another bring rest to both mind and body! Still, as I found it, there was at times absolute "rest" for both mind and body in that blissful repose that only heaven can give.

In but one instance of the manifold letters received was any feeling produced in their perusal except that of pleasure and gratitude that I—with so little physical strength of my own—could bring comfort and pleasure into the lives of others. I thank our gracious Father that he has so kindly permitted it. The one letter to which I refer contains so many almost puerile inquiries, that I simply laid it aside with a quotation from St. Paul, "Of the earth earthy," and asked the Father to lift the heart of the writer into a purer light.

In conclusion I can only reiterate that I am no prophet, I am no seer; but, in my inmost soul, I honestly believe that if the joys of heaven are greater, if the glories "Within the Walls" are more radiant than I in my vision beheld them, I cannot understand how even the immortal spirit can bear to look upon them.

R. R. S.

Made in the USA
Coppell, TX
10 September 2020